A SENSE OF HISTORY

The Era of the Second World War

JOSH BROOMAN

LONGMAN

Acknowledgements

We are grateful to the following for permission to reproduce photographs:

Archiv Gerstenberg, page 18 *right*, 48; Bildarchiv Preussicher Kulturbesitz, page 53, 65, 71, 104; *Bristol Evening Post*, page 87; Josh Brooman, page 13 *below left, below right*, 14; Brown Brothers, page 13 *above*; by permission of the Syndics of Cambridge University Library, page 10, 21 *left*, 70; Camera Press, page 32(ILN), 38 *below centre* (IWM), 54 (IWM), 82 (IWM); Culver Pictures, page 109 above; Documentation Francaise, page 58; from The T & V Holt Collection, page 27; Hulton-Deutsch Collection, page 25, 35, 78, 83, 127 *below*; Robert Hunt Library, page 5 *above*, 37, 38 *above left*, 56, 59, 80 *above*; The illustrated London News Picture Library, page 24, 28, 38 *above right*; Imperial War Museum, London, page 6, 8, 9, 41 *below*, 52, 68, 73, 80 *below*, 86, 88, 89, 92, 93, 96, 118, 120, 122; *Jersey Evening Post*, page 63; Kent Messenger Group Newspapers, page 94; National Archives, Washington, page 74; Peter Newark's Military Pictures, page 31, 41 *above*, 42; Panstwowe Museum, Poland, page 102 *below*, 103; Popperfoto, page 50 *below* (James Jarche), 90, 97, 126; Public Record Office, page 50 *above*; PUNCH, page 36; Frank Spooner Pictures, page 109 *below* (Gamma); Suffolk Record Office, page 12; Thames Television, page 38 *below left*; Topham, page 5 *below*, 15, 34, 46, 55, 95, 119; Ullstein Bilderdienst, page 67, 102 *above*; reprinted by kind permission of *Victor*, page 61, 62; Weidenfeld & Nicolson Publishers, page 100 (Weiner Library); AP/Wide World Photos, page 38 *above centre*, 124, 125; Weiner Library, page 101; from *Unforgettable Fire*, Ed. Japanese Broadcastng Corporation, Wildwood House, page 110.

We are unable to trace the copyright holders of the following and would be grateful of any information that would enable us to do so, page 4, 18 *left*, 21 *right*, 38 *below right*, 47, 72 *left*, 72 *right*, 75, 76, 77, 108, 111, 127 *above*.

Cover photograph: Child rescued from bombed building during the war, Popperfoto.

We are indebted to the following for permission to reproduce copyright material;

Frank Cass & Co Ltd for an abridged extract from *A German Protectorate: The Czechs Under Nazi Rule* by Sheila Grant Duff (pub. 1970); Robert Hale Ltd for an abridged extract from *Tank, 40 Hours of Battle* by Ken Tout (pub. 1985); Editions Robert Laffont for an abridged and translated extract from *La grande histoire des Francais sous l'occupation, Vol 3* by Henri Amouroux (pub. 1978).

We have been unable to trace the copyright holders in the following and would appreciate any information that would enable us to do so:

Exorde by Pierre Drieu de la Rochelle (pub. Editions Gallimard 1961) and *La France Allemande, Paroles du Collaborationnisme Francaise, 1939–1945* by Pascal Ory (pub. Editions Gallimard 1977).

Longman Group UK Limited
*Longman House, Burnt Mill, Harlow, Essex, CM20 2JE, England
and Associated Companies throughout the World.*

© Longman Group UK Limited 1993

First published 1993
ISBN 0 582 21683 4

*Typeset in Monotype Lasercomp 12/14 pt Photina
Printed in Great Britain by Butler & Tanner Limited, Frome*

*The publisher's policy is to use paper manufactured
from sustainable forests*

*Designed by Michael Harris
Illustrated by Tony Richardson (The Wooden Ark Studio)
and Kathy Baxendale*

Contents

1

A War to End All War?

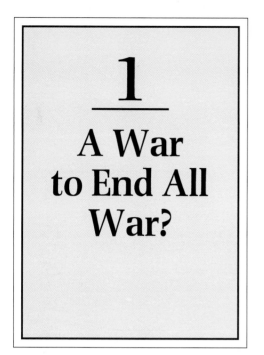

November 1918: a world war is coming to an end. Twenty million people are dead, millions more are wounded. People everywhere are saying it must never happen again. It must be a 'war to end all war'.

September 1939: another world war begins. It will last longer and kill even more people than the first. What has gone wrong? Why a *second* world war only twenty years after the first?

To answer that question we must go back to August 1914, when the First World War was just beginning. On one side were Germany and Austria-Hungary. On the other were Belgium, Britain, France, Russia and Serbia. Many of the soldiers of these countries didn't mind going to war. They were told it would be a short, glorious war – over by Christmas at the latest. Source 1 shows the kind of fighting that many of them expected.

SOURCE 1

An illustration in a German magazine shows British and German soldiers fighting near the Yser canal in Belgium in 1914.
- Find German soldiers wearing pointed *pickelhaube* helmets and British soldiers wearing bearskins and Glengarry caps.
- Find the Union Jack. Who is holding it?
- Which army seems to be winning the battle?

SOURCE 2

British soldiers fire heavy guns at German positions on 12 October 1917. The floodwater in front of them collected when gunfire destroyed drainage ditches in the low-lying farmland of the region.

SOURCE 3

Two British soldiers look at the remains of a German position after it was hit by shell-fire. Find:
- the body of a dead soldier
- the remains of a tree
- scattered cans and pieces of cooking equipment
- churned-up ground and floodwater

activity

1 Look at source 1, then choose five of the following words which you think best describe the kind of fighting in the picture: brave; dangerous; dirty; disgusting; exciting; fair; heroic; patriotic; terrifying; violent; short; long. (Use your own words if you prefer.)
2 Which of the words you have chosen could *not* be used about sources 2 and 3? What words would you use to describe this kind of warfare?

But the war was not over by Christmas. The 'short war' went on for four more years and spread from Europe to thirty countries around the globe. Nor was it a glorious war. The soldiers did not fight heroically on battlefields. Sources 2 and 3, photographs taken during the Third Battle of Ypres in 1917, show the conditions in which millions of them fought.

Why did people turn against the war?

i **Pacifists**   *People who believe that war is wrong and who refuse to fight no matter what the reasons for it are. Pacifists who refused to fight in the First World War were known as conscientious objectors.*

More soldiers died in the First World War than in all previous wars put together (source 6). Most were killed by exploding shells or machine-gun fire. Millions more were badly wounded – mutilated by jagged fragments of exploding shells, blinded by poison gas, crippled by bullets (source 5).

By 1916 many people who had been excited by the war were changing their minds. Some became **pacifists** and opposed it. Source 4 tells us how Sybil Morrison, a 23-year-old ambulance driver, became a pacifist as a result of something she saw one night in 1916 when a German airship was shot down while trying to drop bombs on London.

SOURCE 4

It was roaring flames; blue, red, purple . . . And we knew there were about sixty people in it – we'd always been told there was a crew of about sixty – and that they were being roasted to death. Of course, you weren't supposed to feel any pity for your enemies, nevertheless I was appalled to see the kind, good-hearted British people dancing about in the streets at the sight of sixty people being burned alive – clapping and cheering and singing . . . It was like a flash to me that that was what war did; it created this utter inhumanity in perfectly decent, nice, gentle, kindly people. I just turned my back on it [the war] then.

Sybil Morrison, from a tape-recording made on 13 October 1976

SOURCE 5

Disabled soldiers practise walking with artificial legs at Roehampton hospital in Surrey after the First World War. In Britain alone, almost 2.5 million men received pensions for their wounds after the war – that is, about four in every ten of the soldiers who fought in it.

SOURCE 6

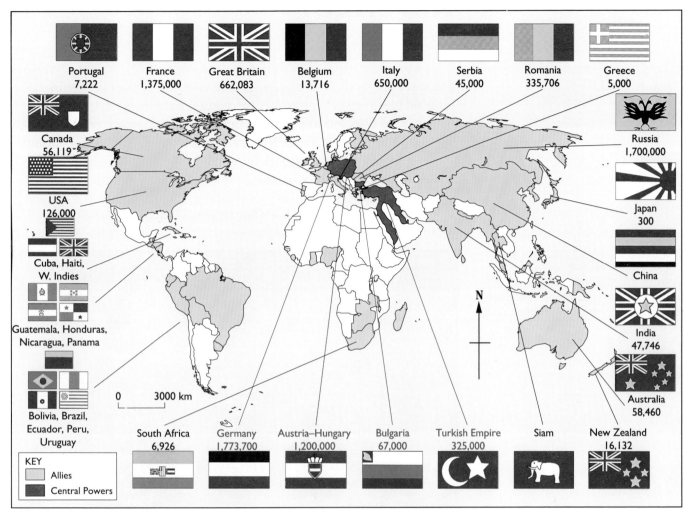

War deaths, 1914–18

By the time Germany surrendered in November 1918, bringing an end to the fighting, people all over the world spoke of the war of 1914–18 as the 'war to end all war'. Many joined anti-war groups to work for a lasting peace. Source 7, a poster put up by wounded ex-soldiers in southern France, was typical of their views.

SOURCE 7

More than 1,700,000 men are dead; over 1,200,000 are mutilated... That's the balance sheet of what was meant to be the 'war to end war'.

We say to every kind of citizen, but especially to fiancées and to mothers, War against War! We say to the millions of soldiers who returned home after their torments, Stand up against War! We openly declare that we, the 'victims of war', are opposed to all wars because ... [we] have been condemned by war to disability and death.

All of us, the mutilated and the crippled, cry out with one heart 'War on War!'

From an ex-soldiers' newspaper, *Le Poilu cévenol* (*The Cévennes Soldier*), 25 March 1921

Revenge

But not everybody turned against the war. Millions of people on both sides wanted revenge for the deaths of their loved ones. One reason why they felt like this was a belief that enemy soldiers committed atrocities. French people read in their newspapers about German soldiers murdering Belgian babies. Germans heard tales of Belgian nurses gouging out the eyes of wounded German soldiers. Italians told stories of Austrian torture, and so on. Source 8 shows what some British people felt about German soldiers in 1918.

SOURCE 8

A poster issued in 1918 by the British Empire Union warns people not to buy goods from German businessmen after the war.

activity

Look carefully at source 8.
1 Find seven scenes in the background of the picture. Describe what is happening in as many of the scenes as you can.
2 Suggest what the artist wanted people to think about the German soldier and businessman.
3 What kind of people in 1918 might have agreed with the artist's point of view? Explain your answer.

activity

4 Look at the speeches in source 9. What do they tell you about:
a why the speakers wanted to punish the Germans?
b how they wanted to punish them?
5 If there had not been an election in 1918, do you think the politicians in source 9 would have said such things? Explain your answer.

In fact, none of those things happened. They were stories that people made up. Even so, by the end of the war in 1918, feelings of hatred and revenge ran deep on both sides. This caused problems for the Allied leaders who had the job of making peace. Public opinion said they should take revenge on the Germans. In Britain, where elections for a new government were due to be held, few politicians dared to disagree. In their speeches in the months before the election, they said such things as:

SOURCE 9

We have to take these people by the throat and let the punishment given to them be an example for generations to come.

Sir George Cave, in the House of Commons on 29 October 1918

Practically the whole German nation was guilty of the crime of aggressive war conducted by brutal and bestial means . . . They were all in it, and they must all suffer for it.

Winston Churchill, speaking in Dundee on 26 November 1918

The Germans, if this government is elected, are going to pay every penny; they are going to be squeezed as a lemon is squeezed – until the pips squeak.

Sir Eric Geddes, speaking in Cambridge on 9 December 1918

SOURCE 10

Watched by the leaders of the Allied countries, two German politicians sign a treaty of peace in the Hall of Mirrors in the palace of Versailles, near Paris, on 28 June 1919. The scene was painted by the British artist Sir William Orpen.

i **Treaty** A written agreement between countries, signed by their leaders, promising to do certain things. A **peace treaty** is usually made at the end of a war, when the defeated country agrees to conditions laid down by the victors.

Making peace

In January 1919, over a thousand politicians from twenty-seven Allied countries met in Paris to make peace with the countries they had beaten – Germany, Austria, Hungary, Bulgaria and Turkey. For the next six months they discussed and debated what to do with their enemies. The result was a series of peace **treaties** (source 10).

The Paris peace treaties began by setting up an organisation called the League of Nations. Its job would be to prevent wars in the future by getting countries to work together peacefully.

To make sure that the defeated countries could not fight again, the treaties said that:

- they must cut the size of their armies and navies
- they must give the Allies money and materials to pay for the cost of repairing damage caused by the fighting
- they must give some of their land to neighbouring countries to make them stronger (source 13).

i | **Reparations** Germany had to give money and goods such as coal to the Allies to help them repair damage done in the Great War. The amount of these reparations was later fixed at £6.6 billion (that is, £6,600,000,000) – about £2,000 billion in today's prices.

The defeated countries complained bitterly that the treaties were unfair. The Germans complained loudest. As source 13 shows, the Treaty of Versailles took away 70,000 square kilometres of land from Germany and gave it to neighbouring countries. It slashed the size of the German army and navy and scrapped its air force. Allied armies were to occupy all parts of Germany west of the River Rhine. German forces were not allowed closer than 50 kilometres to the Rhine.

But what the Germans hated most about the Treaty was that it blamed them for starting the war and therefore ordered them to pay the Allies for the repair of war damage. These payments were known as **reparations**.

When the German people found out what the Treaty said, they reacted angrily. There were mass demonstrations all over the country. A period of national mourning was declared. Places of amusement such as theatres, bars and clubs closed down. A German cartoon (source 12) summed up many people's feelings about the Treaty.

SOURCE 11

activity

1 Look at source 12 and the information in the text.
a What were the main changes that the peace settlement made to the countries beaten in the war?
b Why do you think most Germans complained about the Treaty of Versailles?
2 Source 11 compares the Allied peacemakers with torturers ripping a man's insides out.
a Judging by the information in source 12, why do you think the cartoonist portrayed the peacemakers like this?
b Do you think this was a fair comparison? Explain your answer.
c The cartoon does not picture a real event: the peacemakers did not actually torture anybody. How is the cartoon useful, even though it is about something that did not happen?

A cartoon from a German magazine of 1919 shows Germany as a man being tortured in a dungeon. While the Allied leaders in the background look on, two masked torturers rip out the man's insides.

SOURCE 12

The Paris Peace Settlement of 1919.

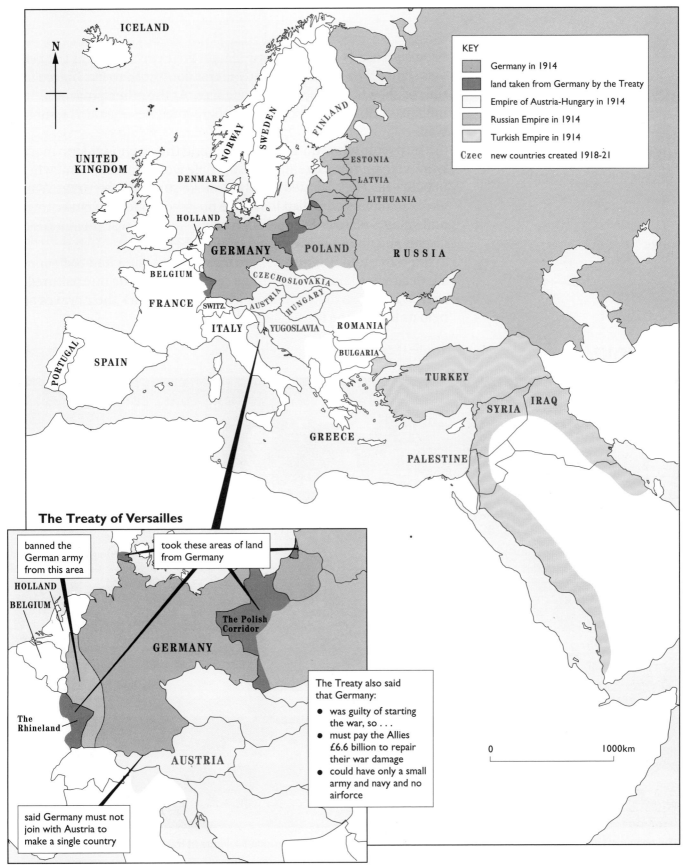

KEY

- Germany in 1914
- land taken from Germany by the Treaty
- Empire of Austria-Hungary in 1914
- Russian Empire in 1914
- Turkish Empire in 1914
- Czec new countries created 1918-21

The Treaty of Versailles

banned the German army from this area

took these areas of land from Germany

The Polish Corridor

The Rhineland

said Germany must not join with Austria to make a single country

The Treaty also said that Germany:

- was guilty of starting the war, so . . .
- must pay the Allies £6.6 billion to repair their war damage
- could have only a small army and navy and no airforce

0   1000km

Remembrance

People's feelings about the war did not go away as soon as the peace was signed. For years to come, millions continued to feel hatred for the people who had been their enemies. At the other extreme, millions continued to believe that there must never again be such a war.

The people who shouted 'revenge' and those who said 'no more war' were on two extremes. Most people were probably somewhere in between. They wanted simply to make sure that the Great War and the soldiers who died in it were never forgotten. In cities, towns and villages all over Europe, such people paid for war memorials to display the names of their dead (source 13).

In France and Belgium, where most of the killing had been done, the dead were laid to rest in huge cemeteries like the one pictured in source 14. More than a million white crosses mark their graves and help us to imagine the awful scale of the killing.

SOURCE 13

The people of the Suffolk village of Stradbrooke pray while a memorial to the dead soldiers of the village is dedicated and unveiled on 30 July 1922.

SOURCE 14

An American war cemetery being built in France shortly after the end of the war. As in the other war cemeteries, all the graves were marked with identical white crosses; families were not allowed to choose their own headstones.

assignments

In the years after the First World War, people everywhere in Britain paid for war memorials to be built. They put up memorials in public places in cities, towns and villages, in churches, clubs, and places of work, and in schools and colleges. The photographs below and overleaf show some common types of memorial.

SOURCE 15a

The most common memorials are stone crosses. They are often found in churchyards, like this one in Frampton-on-Severn in Gloucestershire.

SOURCE 15b

The biggest memorials are often found in town or city centres, like this one in Bristol city centre.

assignments

SOURCE 16c

Some memorials are inside parish churches. This one is in Horfield parish church in Bristol.

SOURCE 16d

Most boys' public schools have memorials. This one was built as a gatehouse for Clifton College in Bristol.

Find a war memorial near your home. You are most likely to find one in or near the parish church. They can also be found in large railway stations, factories, town halls and public schools. When you find a memorial, study it carefully and make notes about what you see. Here are some suggestions about what to look for:

● How many local people died in the Great War of 1914–18?
● Do any names appear more than once? Which? What might they have had in common?
● Does it give the ranks (e.g. Private, Lieutenant, Captain) of those who died? What are they? Which was the most common?
● In which of the armed forces (army, navy, air force) did the men serve? To which did most belong?
● Does it have any writing on it apart from the names of the dead? If so, what?
● Where is it? Why do you think it was put in that particular place?

Now answer these questions:

1 The memorial can be used as a piece of historical evidence. What kind of questions could it help you to answer?

2 What does the memorial tell you about how the Great War affected the local area?

3 Compare your notes with those of two or three other students in the class. What similarities are there between the memorials you have all studied?

4 The memorials you have studied cannot by themselves tell you everything about the effects of the war on the locality. What else would you need to find out if you were researching the effects of the war on the locality?

5 What other kinds of evidence would you look for to add to your information? Which of these would you expect to be the most useful?

<table>
<tr><td>

2
Peace in the Balance, 1919–35

</td><td>

Hopes for a lasting peace

SOURCE 1

I do not think there is the slightest prospect of any war . . . There has scarcely ever been a period in the world's history when war seemed less likely than it does at present.

Lord Cecil, President of the League of Nations Union, speaking in September 1931

You might think that was a foolish claim for anyone to make. But the man who made it generally knew what he was talking about. He had helped set up the League of Nations and was respected in many countries. What reasons could he have had for talking like that in 1931?

The League of Nations

First and foremost, Lord Cecil may have been thinking about what the League of Nations had achieved in the previous ten years. The League, as you have read, was created in 1920 to keep the peace between nations and to get them to work together on international problems. Since its creation, the League had achieved a great deal.

SOURCE 2

</td></tr>
</table>

i **Lord Cecil** Robert Cecil (1864–1958) was a British politician. While a government minister during the First World War, he suggested creating a world organisation to prevent wars from starting in future. At the end of the war he took a leading role in setting up such an organisation – the League of Nations. From 1923 to 1938 he was President of the League of Nations Union, an anti-war organisation that supported the League.

A meeting of the Assembly of the League of Nations in 1924. The Assembly's job was to discuss matters of world concern and to express 'world public opinion'. Each member country sent three delegates to the Assembly each year.
● Look at the colour and gender of the delegates in the picture. What does this tell you about this world assembly?

SOURCE 3

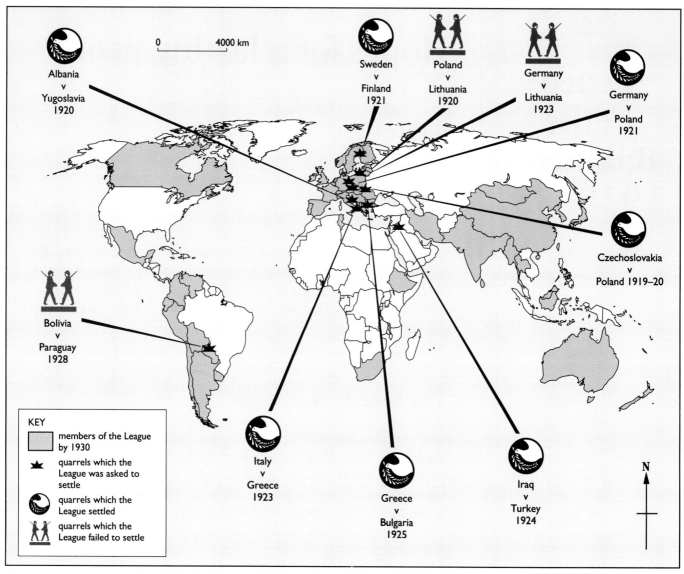

Disputes between countries which the League of Nations was asked to settle during its first ten years.

activity

Study source 3 carefully.
1a How many disputes between countries did the League try to settle in the 1920s?
b How many disputes did it succeed in settling?
2 How does source 3 help to explain why Lord Cecil (source 1) thought there was no likelihood of war in 1931?

It had taken steps to settle ten quarrels between countries (source 3) and it had tried to overcome several international problems. For example, it set up a world Health Organisation to try to wipe out diseases like leprosy and smallpox. Other organisations run by the League tried to improve people's working conditions, to stop drug smuggling and to help homeless refugees. It also had a law court to try legal disputes between countries.

Lord Cecil might also have been thinking about various agreements nations had made with each other since the Great War. In 1925, France, Belgium and Germany had signed the Locarno Pact, promising not to fight each other again. In 1929, sixty-five countries signed an agreement never to use war as a way of settling quarrels between them. Sixty countries had also agreed to meet in Geneva in 1932 for a disarmament conference. There they would talk about reducing their armed forces and their weapons.

Threats to world peace

Not everyone agreed with what Lord Cecil said in 1931. A series of events over the previous two years made it unlikely that the peace could last. Most worryingly, the world had entered a deep economic depression.

The Great Depression was a world-wide economic slump lasting from 1929 until about 1935. During these years, trade between nations dropped. Hundreds of banks closed down. Thousands of companies went out of business. Around 25 million people lost their jobs. Many of the people who lost their jobs also lost their homes. Most of the unemployed spent the Great Depression in terrible poverty.

The Great Depression

The Great Depression of the 1930s put millions of people out of work. In Germany, for example, at least six million workers out of a population of 64 million were unemployed by 1933. Life for the unemployed was very hard. For most, the first result of losing their jobs was hunger. Source 4 shows what one Austrian family had to eat for breakfast, lunch and evening meal (B, L, E) during a week in 1930. The family was taking part in a survey on the effects of unemployment.

SOURCE 4

Monday
B   coffee, bread
L   pea soup, Griesschmarrn*
E   coffee, bread with lard

Tuesday
B   coffee, bread
L   cabbage, potatoes
E   cabbage

Wednesday
B   coffee, bread
L   potato soup, krautfleckerln†
E   coffee, bread

Thursday
B   coffee, bread
L   potato goulash
E   potato goulash

Friday
B   coffee, bread
L   soup, potato noodles
E   coffee, bread

Saturday
B   coffee, bread
L   potato soup, beans
E   coffee, bread

Sunday
B   coffee, white bread
L   soup, sweet noodles
E   coffee, white bread

* cream of wheat with raisins, fried
† fried noodles with spiced cabbage

Diet sheet kept by an unemployed family in the Austrian town of Marienthal, 1930

Hunger and unemployment changed the way people thought and behaved. Out-of-work men were prepared to do almost anything to get work (source 5). Many blamed the government for their poverty and started supporting politicians who promised to give them work

activity

3a Look at source 4. What were the main foods in this family's diet?
b What kinds of food are missing from their diet?
c How might a diet like this affect a family's health?
4a In general, what connections are there between what you eat and the way you feel about life?
b How might living for years on the diet in source 4 have affected the way the family felt about:
(i) themselves, (ii) the government?

SOURCE 5

A German news photographer took this picture in a dole office in 1932. According to his notes, the man was saying, 'We don't want unemployment pay, we don't want social security, we just want some kind of work, road-making, clearing land, anything.'

if they were elected to power (source 6). This German worker explained why he started supporting the National Socialist (or Nazi) Party during the Depression.

SOURCE 7

Thousands of factories closed their doors. Hunger was the daily companion of the German worker ... for no German family received more than 20 to 30 pfennigs dole per head ... Many an honest worker had to resort to theft to obtain food. A case in point is the extensive pilfering of potatoes all through the harvest time ... All fellow citizens yearned for better times. As for me, like many others, I had lost all I possessed ... so, early in 1930, I joined the National Socialist Party.

Theodor Abel, *Why Hitler Came into Power*, 1938

The Nazi party won six and a half million votes in an election for the German Parliament in 1930. The more people lost their jobs, the better the Nazis did in elections. In 1932, the worst year of the Depression with at least six million out of work, the Nazis got 13.5 million votes. This made them the biggest party in the German Parliament. The next year, 1933, the Nazi leader Adolf Hitler became the head of the German government.

SOURCE 6

A Nazi party election poster. It says 'Against Hunger and Despair! Vote for Hitler!'

activity

1 Political posters try to get people to support a particular party. What kinds of people do you think source 6 was designed to appeal to?

2 How does source 6 help to explain why the man in source 7 joined the National Socialist Party?

The spread of dictatorship

Similar things happened in other countries hit by the Depression. Voters blamed their governments for unemployment, and supported parties which promised them jobs. As a result, new governments came to power in more than twenty countries during the 1930s.

In many of these countries, the new leaders who took control ruled as dictators. Source 8 explains what a dictator was and shows

activity

3 Look at source 8 and read what the words 'democracy' and 'dictatorship' mean. Which word best describes the country you live in?
4 Look at the map. How many countries became dictatorships after the Great Depression began in 1929?

SOURCE 8

The spread of dictatorship in the 1930s.

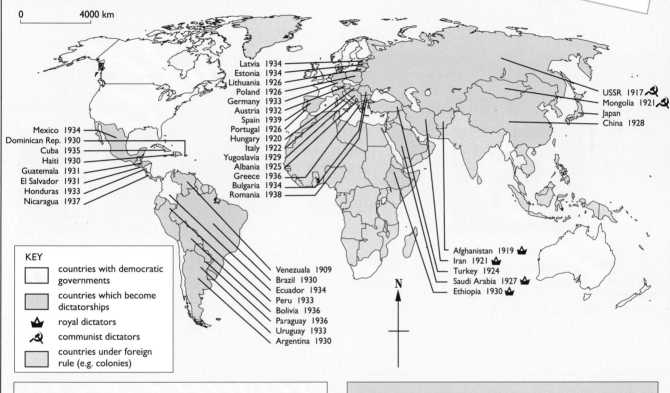

Mexico 1934		USSR 1917
Dominican Rep. 1930		Mongolia 1921
Cuba 1935		Japan
Haiti 1930		China 1928
Guatemala 1931	Latvia 1934	
El Salvador 1931	Estonia 1934	
Honduras 1933	Lithuania 1926	
Nicaragua 1937	Poland 1926	
	Germany 1933	
	Austria 1932	
	Spain 1939	
	Portugal 1926	
	Hungary 1920	
	Italy 1922	
	Yugoslavia 1929	
	Albania 1925	
	Greece 1936	
	Bulgaria 1934	
	Romania 1938	

Venezuela 1909
Brazil 1930
Ecuador 1934
Peru 1933
Bolivia 1936
Paraguay 1936
Uruguay 1933
Argentina 1930

Afghanistan 1919
Iran 1921
Turkey 1924
Saudi Arabia 1927
Ethiopia 1930

KEY

☐ countries with democratic governments

▨ countries which become dictatorships

♛ royal dictators

☭ communist dictators

▩ countries under foreign rule (e.g. colonies)

N

Democracy

In a democracy, people have a say in how the country is governed:

- They vote in regular elections in which there are several parties to choose from.
- They are represnted by the organisations they elect – for example, parliament, or local councils.

In a democracy, people have certain basic rights:

- Freedom of speech (the right to say what they think).
- Freedom of information (the right to read, listen and watch what they want).
- Freedom of belief (the right to worship freely in their own religion).
- Freedom in law (the right to a fair trial if arrested; freedom from unfair arrest).
- Freedom of association (the right to join or form a political party, trade union or other association).

Dictatorship

In a country governed by a dictator, people do not have a say in how the country is run:

- There are no regular elections. Only one party is allowed – the one led by the dictator.
- People are represented only by organisations which the dictator allows to exist.

In a dictatorship people have very few rights:

- There is no free speech. If they criticise the dictator or his party they are likely to be arrested.
- There is no freedom of information. The dictator controls the press, books, film etc.
- Not all religions are allowed.
- There is no legal freedom. The police can arrest who they like and keep them in prison without trial.
- People can only join associations allowed by the dictator.

SOURCE 9

Four dictators and their parties.

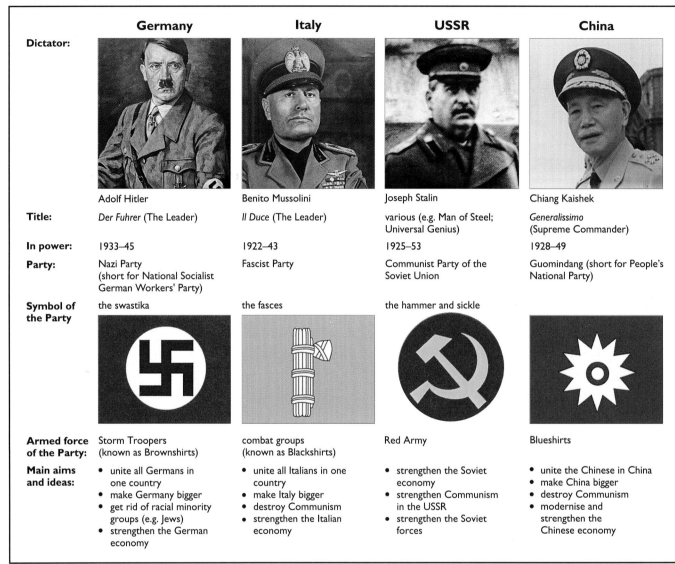

	Germany	Italy	USSR	China
Dictator:	Adolf Hitler	Benito Mussolini	Joseph Stalin	Chiang Kaishek
Title:	*Der Fuhrer* (The Leader)	*Il Duce* (The Leader)	various (e.g. Man of Steel; Universal Genius)	*Generalissimo* (Supreme Commander)
In power:	1933–45	1922–43	1925–53	1928–49
Party:	Nazi Party (short for National Socialist German Workers' Party)	Fascist Party	Communist Party of the Soviet Union	Guomindang (short for People's National Party)
Symbol of the Party	the swastika	the fasces	the hammer and sickle	
Armed force of the Party:	Storm Troopers (known as Brownshirts)	combat groups (known as Blackshirts)	Red Army	Blueshirts
Main aims and ideas:	• unite all Germans in one country • make Germany bigger • get rid of racial minority groups (e.g. Jews) • strengthen the German economy	• unite all Italians in one country • make Italy bigger • destroy Communism • strengthen the Italian economy	• strengthen the Soviet economy • strengthen Communism in the USSR • strengthen the Soviet forces	• unite the Chinese in China • make China bigger • destroy Communism • modernise and strengthen the Chinese economy

countries around the world which became dictatorships in the 1920s and 1930s. Source 9 compares four of the leading dictators and shows how they ran their countries in very similar ways.

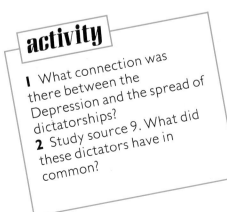

activity

1 What connection was there between the Depression and the spread of dictatorships?

2 Study source 9. What did these dictators have in common?

What was it like to live in a dictatorship?

The most powerful of the dictators was Adolf Hitler. After becoming head of the German government in 1933, he banned all political parties other than his own Nazi Party. His private army of 'Brownshirts' rounded up thousands of his opponents and threw them into prison. Even leading Nazis who disagreed with his views were killed. By mid-1934 there was no one in Germany to stop him doing what he wanted.

Hitler and the Nazis had three main aims:

- to get Germany out of the Depression
- to make Germany powerful again
- to create a 'pure German' society by getting rid of racial minority groups such as Jews.

To achieve these aims quickly the Nazis needed total control of the German people, a task that was shared by the Nazi Party and the police. Local Party officials – 400,000 of them – kept watch on every street and every block of flats in every town and city. They snooped on people and reported suspicious behaviour to the police.

The Nazis also controlled people through Party organisations. Boys and girls, for example, had to belong to Nazi youth organisations such as the Hitler Youth. In these organisations, young people were taught to accept Nazi ideas without question.

Whether or not people belonged to the Party, the Nazis tried to control their thinking. The government controlled the media – newspapers, films, radio, plays, cinema and books – and made sure they put across Nazi ideas. The government even restricted the activities of the churches and set up its own Nazi church.

Above all, people had to show respect for and obedience to Hitler and the Nazis. Portraits of Hitler (source 10) were mass produced and hung up in school rooms, government offices, law courts and every other public place. The swastika flag of the Nazi Party hung from every flagpole. Government workers had to salute each other with outstretched arms and say 'Heil Hitler' (source 11).

SOURCE 10

Ein Volk, ein Reich, ein Führer

An official portrait of Hitler painted in 1936. The words mean 'One People, One *Reich*, One Leader' (*Reich* means 'empire', in this case Germany).

SOURCE 11

Office workers and customers in a Munich bank give 'the Hitler salute' as they listen to a speech by Hitler on a public radio.

Source 12 shows how difficult it was to avoid doing so. It was written by a member of the Communist Party, which opposed the Nazis.

SOURCE 12

For three months I had managed to avoid saluting the swastika flag . . . I tried it once too often, however . . . I caught sight of an approaching procession of Nazi nurses, carrying banners. Without stopping to think, I turned my back on it and walked in the opposite direction, only to face four Brownshirts crossing towards me from the other side of the street.

'Trying to get out of it?' said one. 'Arm up! And now – ?'

'Heil Hitler,' I said.

I could have spat at myself as I strode past the procession with arm uplifted.

Karl Billinger, *All Quiet in Germany*, 1935

Why did Karl Billinger give the Nazi salute when he didn't want to? One reason can be guessed from source 13. It is part of a Communist Party pamphlet describing how the Brownshirts treated Communists in 1933.

SOURCE 13

In Berlin alone thousands of Socialist and Communist officials were dragged from their beds at night . . . and led away to Brownshirt barracks. There they were worked over with boot and whip, beaten with steel rods and rubber truncheons until they collapsed unconscious . . . Many were forced to drink castor oil or had urine directed into their mouths. Others had their bones broken.

From *Listen! Read! Pass it on! Hitler's Crimes*, an underground pamphlet circulated by Communists in 1933

---

activity

1 Look at the aims of the Nazis listed on page 21. Take each aim in turn and say why you think German people might have agreed with it.

2 Look at source 11 and read sources 12 and 13. Suppose that someone in that group of people in the bank opposed Hitler and decided not to give the salute:

a What do you think might have happened to him or her?

b Do you think it would have been more sensible (i) to salute and say nothing against Hitler, or (ii) not salute and show disapproval of Hitler? Explain your answer.

3a Discuss your answers to 1 and 2 with another group or pair.

b Organise a class discussion about why you think many German people supported and obeyed the Nazi party.

Aggression

The spread of dictatorship was a threat to world peace because some dictators started to act aggressively towards other countries. They did so in an attempt to improve the situation in their own countries.

As source 14 shows, world peace was threatened by a series of attacks and invasions during the 1930s. Japan attacked both China and the Soviet Union. Italy invaded Ethiopia, hoping to add land to the Italian empire. Germany grabbed land from its neighbours. Several countries sent armies to Spain to help Spaniards fight each other in a civil war.

SOURCE 14

Acts of aggression in the 1930s.

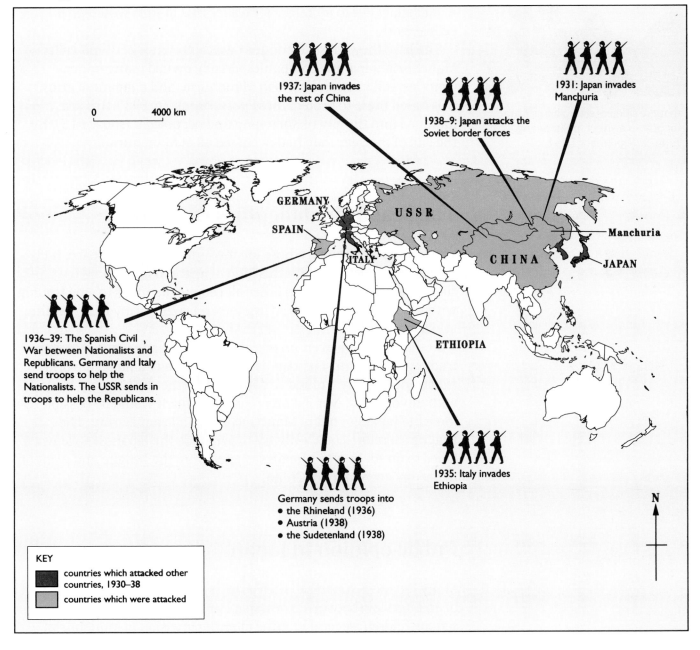

0   4000 km

1937: Japan invades the rest of China

1938–9: Japan attacks the Soviet border forces

1931: Japan invades Manchuria

GERMANY

USSR

SPAIN

Manchuria

ITALY

CHINA

JAPAN

1936–39: The Spanish Civil War between Nationalists and Republicans. Germany and Italy send troops to help the Nationalists. The USSR sends in troops to help the Republicans.

ETHIOPIA

Germany sends troops into
● the Rhineland (1936)
● Austria (1938)
● the Sudetenland (1938)

1935: Italy invades Ethiopia

N

KEY
countries which attacked other countries, 1930–38
countries which were attacked

How did Japan's aggression affect hopes for peace?

SOURCE 15

Japanese soldiers set up a machine gun post in a street in Shenyang, China, in September 1931.

Japan was the first country to act aggressively. Japan had been hit badly by the Depression. Half her factories were shut and millions of people were close to starvation. The Government was slow to help these people and this had made it unpopular.

Young officers in the Japanese army hated the Government for doing so little. They decided to take matters into their own hands. They thought that the quickest way out of the Depression would be to conquer foreign land. This would give Japan raw materials and would allow her to increase her trade. This in turn would give people work.

The land they chose to conquer was a province of China called Manchuria. Japanese companies already owned many mines, factories, railways and ports in Manchuria, and a Japanese army was based there to protect these possessions. In 1931 this army marched into the city of Shenyang and occupied it (source 15). By the end of the year they had occupied all of Manchuria.

The League in difficulties

The League of Nations, whose job it was to keep world peace, had three ways of dealing with this kind of aggression. It could try simple persuasion. It could order all League members to stop trading with the attacker. Or it could organise a League army to throw the attacker out.

In this case, however, no member of the League wanted to stop trading with Japan. The Depression had already damaged world trade, and nobody wanted to damage it further by banning trade with anyone else. Nor did any member think it would be possible to force the Japanese out of Manchuria with a League army. The League therefore could only try to persuade the Japanese to leave. It failed to do so. In 1933 Japan resigned from the League and went on to occupy even more of China.

Public opinion in Japan

Many Japanese supported their army's attack on China. Here is part of an interview between a newspaper reporter and some Japanese schoolchildren, several months after the invasion of Manchuria:

activity

1 Source 16 tells us what some Japanese schoolchildren thought about their army's invasion of China. Why might a supporter of peace in the 1930s have found their views very worrying?

2 Look at sources 16 and 17. How do you think the children in source 16 might have described the people in source 17? Explain your answer.

SOURCE 16

Interviewer: *What is the Manchurian incident all about?*

Kato: *The Chinese insulted us and our soldiers are fighting them in Manchuria to avenge it.*

Interviewer: *The League of Nations has been making quite a fuss recently. What do you think of the League?*

Kato: *It's a place where the cowards of the world get together to talk.*

Interviewer: *If you were Foreign Minister, what would you do?*

Nakajima: *The League of Nations is biased, so I wouldn't have anything to do with it . . .*

'Round-table discussion of Elementary School Students', *Asahi Gurafu* (a Japanese newspaper), 1 January 1932

Public opinion in Europe

In Europe, many people were worried by the League's failure to halt Japan's invasion of Manchuria. They feared it would lead to more aggression in the future. Hoping to avoid this, anti-war groups mounted campaigns to turn public opinion against war (source 17).

SOURCE 17

Women and children get ready to march through London on an anti-war demonstration in 1931. Find:
- banners with the olive branch symbol and the word PAX (Latin For Peace)
- white flowers, symbolising peace.

In Britain, millions of ordinary people were able to express their feelings about war. In 1934, Canon Dick Sheppard, the leader of an anti-war group called the Peace Pledge Union, appealed to people who felt like him to send him a postcard, stating that they disagreed with war and would never fight in one. Within a year he received 80,000 postcards, many from ex-servicemen, saying that they agreed.

Later in 1934, Lord Cecil organised a nationwide 'peace ballot' in which people were asked to vote on whether they supported the League and whether they agreed with disarmament. Nearly half the adults in Britain voted – 11.5 million people. Eleven million said they supported the League and 10 million were in favour of disarmament.

assignments

1 Here are two reasons why many people in the 1920s thought there would be a lasting peace after the Great War.

● Many countries had signed agreements promising never to go to war again.

● Sixty countries had agreed to meet for a disarmament conference in Geneva.

Using the information in Part 2, give at least one more reason why many people expected peace to last.

2 Below, in no particular sequence, is a set of five developments in world affairs. Rearrange them into a sequence that would explain why world peace was threatened after 1929.

A   New leaders came to power in twenty countries during the Depression.

B   Many unemployed people stopped supporting their governments and voted for parties which promised them jobs.

C   The Depression led to mass unemployment and a drop in world trade.

D   Some of the new leaders who came to power during the Depression were dictators.

E   Three dictators tried to solve their countries' problems by using force to take land and resources from other countries.

3a Put the developments in the list above into the following categories: political developments, social developments, economic developments. (Some might be put into more than one group).
b Which category of developments do you think was most important in undermining world peace? Explain your answer.

4 'If the Depression had not happened, there would have been no threat to world peace in the 1930s.' Explain carefully whether you think this statement is true or false.

3
War Clouds Gather, 1936–39

You found out in Part 2 that world peace was threatened when some countries started acting aggressively during the Great Depression. First Japan invaded Manchuria in 1931, then Italy invaded Abyssinia in 1935. The next country to use aggression was Germany, led by Adolf Hitler.

Nazi expansion

Hitler had three aims in his dealings with other countries. The first was to get back the land which the Versailles Treaty took from Germany in 1919. The second was to have all German-speaking people living in one country. The third was to make Germany bigger by taking land from countries to the east.

He began by building up Germany's armed forces, even though this was forbidden by the Versailles Treaty. In 1935 he ordered that all men must do military service for two years when they reached 18. The armed forces thus grew from 100,000 in 1933 to 500,000 in 1936. Source 1 shows one reason why Hitler wanted to break the Treaty in this way.

SOURCE 1

This German postcard was produced in 1935, shortly after Hitler introduced compulsory military service.

Germany's Disarmament and the Armament of her Neighbours

activity

1 Look at source 1.
a Explain what point you think the postcard was trying to make.
b Suggest why this German postcard was in English rather than German.
c How does source 1 help to explain why Hitler wanted to have soldiers in the Rhineland?

SOURCE 2

This photograph, taken in March 1936, shows German troops entering Cologne, a major city in the Rhineland.

Hitler used his new forces to occupy the Rhineland area of Germany (shown in source 1). This too was forbidden by the Versailles Treaty which said that the German army must not go within 50 kilometres of the River Rhine. Many Germans hated the ban. It hurt their national pride and it left their country open to attack. In 1936 Hitler sent 32,000 soldiers to occupy the Rhineland (source 2).

activity

1 Look at source 2. Judging by this photograph, how well equipped were the German soldiers who occupied the Rhineland? Explain your answer.

Why did Britain not stop the Rhineland occupation?

Hitler risked starting a war by occupying the Rhineland. The Treaty said that the Allies could use armed force to stop Germany doing so. However, the chiefs of the French army warned that a million soldiers would be needed to expel the Germans from the Rhineland. The French government, which had many other problems to deal with, did not want to risk doing this without Britain's support.

The British government, however, decided not to take action. It was not convinced that German soldiers in the Rhineland were a threat to peace. Hitler said on the day he sent his army into the Rhineland:

SOURCE 3

We proclaim now more than ever before our wish to further the cause of understanding between the nations of Europe . . . In Europe we have no territorial claims to put forward.

Adolf Hitler, *Speech in the Reichstag (German Parliament)*, 7 March 1936

A group of influential people known as the **Cliveden set** believed Hitler's words. One of them, Lord Lothian, said:

SOURCE 4

After all, the Germans are only going into their own back garden.

Lord Lothian, *The Lothian Papers*

The Cliveden set did all they could to convince the British government of this. On the day after the Rhineland occupation, they gathered at Lord Lothian's house to discuss 'How to deal with Hitler'. One, a close friend of the Prime Minister, wrote in his diary:

SOURCE 5

I went this morning for a walk with Toynbee, most of the others going to play golf. Toynbee has just returned from a visit to Germany . . . He had an interview with Hitler which lasted one and three quarter hours. He is convinced of his sincerity in desiring peace in Europe . . . I have asked Toynbee to put his impressions down and shall have them typed here and handed to S. B. [Stanley Baldwin, the Prime Minister] and Eden [the Foreign Minister] first thing in the morning. What I am trying to secure is that S. B. should have his mind made up on . . . accepting Hitler at face value and trying him out fairly . . . One wants S. B's mind firmly made up before he enters the Cabinet where he will encounter all sorts of contradictory advice.

Thomas Jones, *A Diary With Letters*, 1954

The following day, Eden told Parliament in a long speech that Britain would not take action against Germany. He said:

SOURCE 6

There is, I am thankful to say, no reason to suppose that the present German action implies a threat of hostilities. The German government speak of their 'unchangeable longing for a real pacification of Europe' and express a willingness to conclude a non-aggression pact with France and Belgium.

Parliamentary Debates, 9 March 1936

---

i The **Cliveden set** was a group of fashionable and influential people who socialised at the country estate of Lord and Lady Astor at Cliveden in Berkshire. They included leading newspaper editors, politicians, bankers and academics. The members mentioned here were Lord Lothian, a politician, the historian Arnold Toynbee, and Tom Jones, a close friend and adviser of the Prime Minister.

activity

2 Explain in your own words Lord Lothian's comment in source 4.

3 Look at source 5.

a The Cabinet is the group of senior ministers, headed by the Prime Minister, who decide what the government should do. Why do you think Thomas Jones wanted to tell Stanley Baldwin and Eden about his discussion with Toynbee *before* the Cabinet met the next morning?

b What does source 5 suggest about the way in which the Government decided what to do about the Rhineland occupation?

4 Use sources 1, 3, 4, 5 and 6 to suggest why Britain did not take action to expel the German army from the Rhineland.

Union with Austria, 1938

Hitler's next aim was to make Germany and Austria, where most people were German-speakers, into a single country. Although many people in both countries wanted it, this too was forbidden by the Versailles Treaty, so Hitler had to go about it carefully.

He began by ordering Austrian Nazis to make trouble by letting off bombs and organising riots. He wanted it to look as if the Austrian government could not control the country. As Hitler intended, the Austrian police could not halt the violence, so he said he would send the German army into Austria to 'restore order'. The Austrian leader protested but could not find a way of protecting his country from Hitler's threat. He therefore resigned. An Austrian Nazi took his place and immediately asked Hitler to send troops to 'restore order'. The German army thus marched into Austria by invitation. Soon after, Hitler announced that Germany and Austria were a single country called 'Greater Germany'.

Takeover of Czechoslovakia, 1938–39

Hitler used the same trick to get hold of the Sudetenland area of Czechoslovakia, where three million German-speaking people lived. He ordered his supporters there to stage riots and demonstrations to make it look as if the Czech government could not control the Sudetenland. Hitler then sent the German army to the Czech border and demanded that the Czechs hand over the area to Germany.

The Czechs refused, and prepared to defend themselves. They could count not only on a strong army but also on support promised by France and the USSR if they were ever attacked. It looked as if a German attack on Czechoslovakia would lead to a war involving many countries.

However, the leaders of Britain and France did not want war. Britain's Prime Minister, Neville Chamberlain, flew to Germany to discuss the matter with Hitler. Hitler told him that the Sudetenland was the last piece of land he wanted. Chamberlain and Hitler, along with the leaders of France and Italy, then met in Munich for a conference to settle the matter. They agreed that the Czechs should give the Sudetenland to Germany. The Czechs had no choice but to agree to this. If they did not agree, they would have to fight Germany alone. So Czech frontier guards left their posts on 1 October 1938 and allowed the German army to march into the Sudetenland.

For a while it looked as if there would be peace in Europe. But Hitler had lied to Chamberlain. The Sudetenland was not the last piece of land he wanted. Six months later, in 1939, his army marched into the rest of Czechoslovakia. Half the country was made into part of Germany, and the other half into a new state called Slovakia. Source 8 shows what Germany now looked like.

SOURCE 7

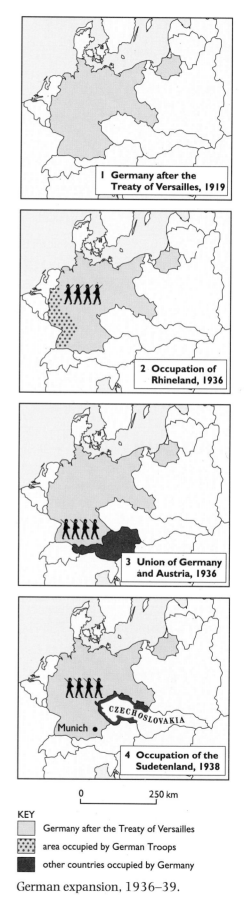

KEY

Germany after the Treaty of Versailles

area occupied by German Troops

other countries occupied by Germany

German expansion, 1936–39.

SOURCE 8

A German poster of 1939 shows the new shape of Greater Germany (*Grossdeutschland*) in 1939.

activity

Compare this map of Germany in 1939 with the map showing Germany in 1919 on page 11 (source 12).

1 Describe three ways in which the shape of Germany changed between 1919 and 1939.

2 Using Part 3, explain how those changes came about.

Was Chamberlain wrong to talk to Hitler?

When you make a mistake, it's often easy to look back and see where you went wrong. This is called having hindsight. It's much harder to tell in advance when you are going to make a mistake.

Some events in history are like this. With hindsight, it can seem obvious to us that someone was making a mistake. One such event was the Munich Agreement of 1938. With hindsight, it seems obvious that Hitler had no intention of keeping his promises and that Chamberlain should have helped the Czechs fight Hitler instead

SOURCE 9

Neville Chamberlain arrives in Munich in October 1938 to discuss the Czech crisis with Hitler.

of talking with him. Even at the time there were many people who thought he should do so:

SOURCE 10

[Man, age 70] I think he [Chamberlain]'s doing wrong . . . Why shouldn't the Czechs fight for their country? Why should we allow a bully like Hitler to dominate Europe? Let's fight him and finish it.

[Bus conductor, age 30] What the hell's he got the right to go over there and do a dirty trick like that. It'll have the whole world against us now. Who'll trust us?

[Woman, age 32] It's a low-down dirty deal. It gives lots of them Czechs over to Hitler.

Street interviews recorded by **Mass Observation** in London on 20 September 1938

Why wouldn't Chamberlain help the Czechs to fight Germany? One reason can be found in a speech he made that summer:

SOURCE 11

When I think of those four terrible years and I think of the 7 million young men who were cut off in their prime, the 13 million who were maimed and mutilated, the misery and the suffering of the mothers and fathers, the sons and daughters of those who were killed, and the wounded, then I am bound to say . . . in war . . . there are no winners, but all are losers. It is those thoughts which have made me . . . strain every nerve to avoid a repetition of the Great War in Europe.

Neville Chamberlain, speaking in Kettering on 2 July 1938

It wasn't only memories of the First World War that made Chamberlain hate the idea of war in 1938. Scientists had convinced the government that a second war would be even more horrific than the first because a new kind of weapon would be used to attack their cities: bomber aircraft. A Member of Parliament described the expected horrors of bombing:

SOURCE 12

A week or ten days' intensive bombing attack upon London would be a very serious matter indeed . . . 30 to 40 thousand people would be killed or maimed . . . At least 3 or 4 million would be driven out into the open country around the metropolis [city]. This vast mass of human beings [would be] without shelter and without food, without sanitation, and without provision for the maintenance of order.

Winston Churchill, speech in the House of Commons on 28 November 1934

While Chamberlain was talking to Hitler in 1938, the British people were asked to prepare defences against an enemy attack with poison gas or high-explosive bombs. Scenes like those in source 13 took place all over the country.

---

i Mass Observation was a group of researchers formed in 1937 to make detailed observations of ordinary people's lives and to find out their opinions. They interviewed many British people during September 1938 to find out what they thought about the Czech crisis.

SOURCE 13

Children at a school in Kent watch workmen building an air raid shelter in the school field during the Munich Crisis, September 1939.

The digging of trenches and the trying-on of gas masks terrified many people. When asked 'What will you actually do if war breaks out?' one woman told an interviewer:

SOURCE 14

I have been collecting poisons for some time . . . I have sufficient to give myself, husband and all the children a lethal dose. I can remember the last war. I don't want to live through another, or the children either. I shan't tell them. I shall just do it.

Interview recorded by *Mass Observation* in September 1938

When Chamberlain returned to Britain from Munich, and announced that there would not be a war, millions of people felt great relief. A middle-aged newspaper columnist summed up their feelings when he wrote:

SOURCE 15

Thanks to Chamberlain, thousands of young men will live. I will live.

Lord Castlerosse, *The Daily Express*, 1 October 1938

When a crowd of happy people gathered outside 10 Downing Street to cheer him, Chamberlain leaned out from an upper window and said:

SOURCE 16

There has come back from Germany to Downing Street peace with honour. I believe it is peace for our time ... And now I recommend you to go home and sleep quietly in your beds.

Illustrated London News, 8 October 1938

SOURCE 17

Neville Chamberlain, with his wife, speaking to the crowd in Downing Street after his return from Munich.

assignments

1 Look at these sources:

A   Source 12 and 13 on page 22   D   Sources 5 and 6 on pages 6 and 7
B   Source 7 on page 30   E   Sources 11 and 12 on page 33
C   Source 10 on page 33   F   Sources 13–15 on page 34

a How do A, B and C help you to understand why many people in Britain wanted to go to war with Germany in 1938?
b How do D, E and F help to explain why many people supported Chamberlain's decision not to go to war with Hitler?

2a Neville Chamberlain told the crowd outside 10 Downing Street 'I recommend you to go home and sleep quietly in your beds.' Judging by sources 12–14, why do you think many people might have found it difficult to get to sleep in the week leading up to this event?
b How likely do you think it was that the crowd Chamberlain spoke to slept soundly that night? Explain your answer carefully.

3 Judging by all you have read, do you think Chamberlain was wrong to talk to Hitler in 1938? Explain your answer carefully.

1939: the storm breaks

SOURCE 18

AN OLD STORY RETOLD

Herr Hitler. "It's all right; you know the proverb—'Barking dogs don't bite'?"

Signor Mussolini. "Oh, yes, I know it, and *you* know it; but does the dog know it?"

A cartoon by Bernard Partridge which appeared in *Punch* magazine in Britain on 5 April 1939.

activity

Look at source 18.
1a Who are the two men in the cartoon?
b Which country does the dog represent?
c Which country is the dog protecting?
d What is the dog threatening to do if the two men go through the gate?
2 What had the dog done the year before to make the men think it would not carry out its threat?
3 Which man is not sure whether to enter? Why do you think he is unsure?

When Hitler occupied Czechoslovakia, he broke the promises he made at Munich. Chamberlain realised that Hitler could not be trusted, and decided that he must be stopped from taking any more land.

It was easy to see which bit of land Hitler would take next. He wanted an area of Poland known as the Polish Corridor which had been taken from Germany in 1919 (see page 11). It was the only piece of land taken in 1919 that Hitler had not yet got back. Chamberlain therefore promised to help defend Poland against Germany. The government of France joined in the promise.

This did not seem to scare Hitler (source 18). He carried on building up his armed forces. Then he made an agreement with the dictator of Italy, Mussolini, that they would help each other in any war. By the summer of 1939, Europe was divided into two enemy camps. Britain and France were in one camp, saying they would protect Poland. Germany and Italy were in the other, and Germany looked certain to attack Poland.

This worried the leader of the Soviet Union, Stalin. He knew that Hitler hated the Soviet Union because it was a communist country, and he knew that Hitler wanted extra land in eastern Europe. He feared that a German attack on Poland would be followed by an attack on his own country. So Stalin looked for help. He offered to join Britain and France in their alliance to protect Poland. But the British and French governments did not trust Stalin. Talks between them quickly broke down.

The Nazi–Soviet Pact

Stalin instead turned for help to the man he trusted least: Hitler. They signed an agreement not to fight each other if there was a war in Poland. In secret, they also promised to divide Poland between them after it had been conquered.

This Nazi–Soviet Pact amazed everyone. Overnight, two enemies had agreed not to fight each other. But their reasons for doing it soon became clear. Stalin signed it so that he could be safe from Germany while he built up his forces. Hitler signed it so that he could attack Poland without having to worry that the Soviet army would stand in his way. Only a week after the two dictators had signed the Pact, the German army invaded Poland. Soviet forces invaded soon after. Between them, they gobbled up the country.

This was the start of a major war. On 3 September, Britain and France honoured their promise to help Poland by declaring war on

Germany. Britain and France were thus at war with Germany and its ally, Italy. And because Britain and France had great empires in Africa, Asia and the Far East, the war would soon spread from Europe to other parts of the world, making it a second world war.

SOURCE 19

German troops enter a town in Poland in September 1939.

assignments

There were many reasons why a second world war began in 1939. Two of the reasons outlined in this chapter are:

A   Hitler acted aggressively towards neighbouring countries because he wanted to get back land taken from Germany in 1919.
B   Britain and France declared war on Germany in 1939 to protect Poland after the German army invaded it.

1 Add as many other causes as you can to this list.

2 Cause A was an underlying, or long-term cause of the war. This means that it went on for a long time before 1939 and did not decide the exact moment when war began. Cause B was a short-term cause, meaning that it happened just before the event and helped trigger it. Add at least one more underlying cause and one more immediate cause to the list.

3 Which of the causes you have listed do you think was the most important? Explain your answer.

4 If one of the causes you have listed had not existed, does this mean that the war would not have happened? Explain your answer.

4
The World at War, 1939–45

Germany conquers Europe

German forces invaded Poland on 1 September 1939. Using a new method of warfare called **blitzkrieg**, they took only a week to smash the Polish army. By November, the Germans and Russians had occupied the whole country. Later, the Russians also took the Baltic States and Finland.

Although Britain and France joined the war to protect Poland, their forces were too far away to stop the invasion. So, for the next eight months, they did no actual fighting but waited and prepared for war. People called this the 'phoney war'.

In the spring of 1940, Hitler's forces attacked and occupied four neutral countries: Denmark, Norway, Belgium and Holland. Then they entered France, where they beat the French army and forced the British army in France to retreat across the Channel from

SOURCE 1

German soldiers advance along a street in a town in Norway.

German soldiers enter the Dutch city of Maastricht during their invasion of Holland.

German troops enter a burning village in Poland.

British soldiers are rescued from Dunkirk after being trapped there in the German invasion of France.

Hitler poses in front of the Eiffel Tower in Paris after his armies had occupied France.

A German Stuka dive bomber drops its bombs to clear the way for tanks on the ground in the invasion of Poland.

SOURCE 2

The German and
Soviet conquest
of Europe, 1939–40.

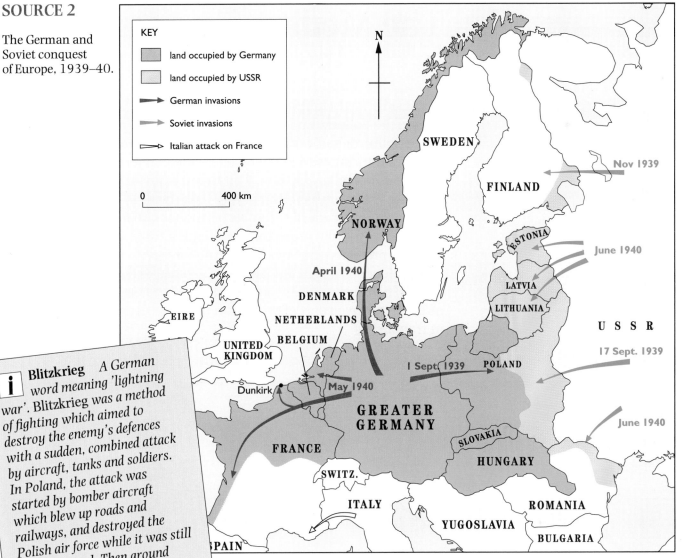

i Blitzkrieg   *A German
word meaning 'lightning
war'. Blitzkrieg was a method
of fighting which aimed to
destroy the enemy's defences
with a sudden, combined attack
by aircraft, tanks and soldiers.
In Poland, the attack was
started by bomber aircraft
which blew up roads and
railways, and destroyed the
Polish air force while it was still
on the ground. Then ground
forces attacked the Polish army,
tanks rolling forward behind the
dive bombers. Finally, soldiers
on trucks and motor-bikes came
to fight any Polish units that
still survived.*

activity

1 Look at the photographs
opposite (source 1). Using
the map (source 2) and the
information on these pages,
work out the order in which
the photographs were taken.
2 Which of the pictures in
source 1 show the German
army using the *Blitzkrieg*
method of warfare?

Dunkirk. Italian forces attacked southern France at the same time.
The French surrendered, and German forces occupied northern
France as well as the British Channel Islands.

Britain was now the only country left to fight Germany. It looked
as if Britain would have to make peace, leaving Germany in control
of Europe. But Britain now had a new Prime Minister, Winston
Churchill, who took over from Neville Chamberlain in May 1940.
Churchill refused to surrender, so Hitler ordered his generals to
prepare an invasion of Britain. Narrowly, the British Air Force
prevented the invasion by defeating German fighter aircraft in a long
air battle known as the Battle of Britain (August–September 1940).

This did not make Britain safe from attack, however. From
7 September 1940 onwards, German bomber aircraft dropped
bombs on many of Britain's towns and cities, trying to destroy
factories, railways, ports and people's homes. These attacks were
known as the 'Blitz'. In reply, British aircraft dropped bombs on
German towns and cities. For nearly five years, this was to be the
main kind of warfare between the two countries.

The Mediterranean war

i **Balkans** Balkan is the Turkish word for mountain. The Balkans are the mountains in south-east Europe and the Balkan states were the countries of that region: Yugoslavia, Albania, Greece, Bulgaria and Romania.

In autumn 1940 fighting spread to two areas in the Mediterranean region: the **Balkans** and North Africa (source 3).

Mussolini, dictator of Italy and ally of Hitler, wanted to make Italy rich by capturing land in the Mediterranean region. The British were determined to stop him. The Mediterranean was a vital shipping route between Britain and its oil fields in the Persian Gulf. Britain could not afford to lose its oil supplies, so navy bases at Gibraltar and Malta protected the shipping route, and British forces in Egypt protected the Suez Canal (source 5).

In October 1940 the Italian army invaded Greece. Their attack failed. The Greeks quickly drove them back. Shortly after, British aircraft destroyed part of the Italian navy at Taranto. Mussolini was in trouble.

SOURCE 3

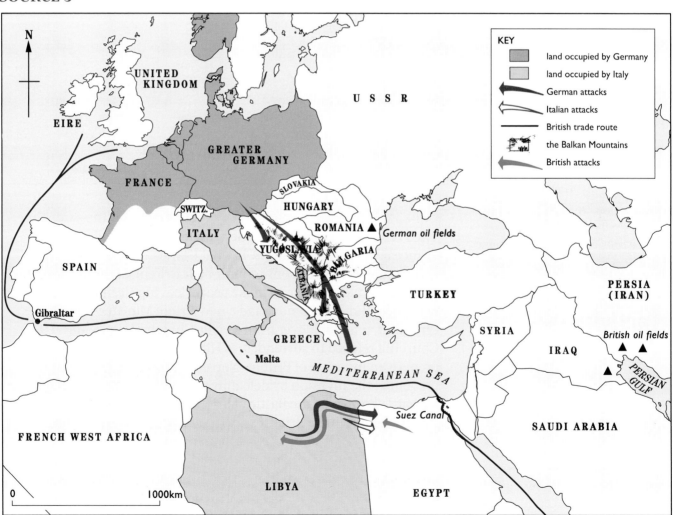

The Mediterranean region, 1940–41.

SOURCE 4

A British poster of 1941 shows one reason why the war was a world war: soldiers from many of Britain's colonies and dominions joined in the fighting against Germany and Italy in the Mediterranean war.

THE BRITISH COMMONWEALTH OF NATIONS

TOGETHER

SOURCE 5

A British bomber aircraft flies over one of the pyramids in Egypt.

activity

1 Look at source 4.
a Find soldiers from Britain, Canada and Australia in the poster.
b What other nationalities can you find?
c What did these nationalities have in common at the time of the Second World War?
2 If Britain and Germany had had their own sources of oil in 1940–41, how might this have changed the war between them?

These British and Greek victories alarmed Hitler. He feared that the British would now set up air force bases in Greece and bomb the oil fields in Romania where Germany got most of its oil. So Hitler decided to bring the whole Balkan region under his control. He put pressure on the Balkan countries to become his allies. Three – Hungary, Romania and Bulgaria – agreed, but Yugoslavia refused. Hitler therefore sent German forces into Yugoslavia and occupied the country. German troops occupied Greece at the same time. By spring 1941 the entire Balkan region was under German control.

On the other side of the Mediterranean there was fighting in North Africa. German and Italian troops fought battles against soldiers from Britain, Australia, India and New Zealand (source 4). Their aim was to cut off Britain's oil supplies through the Suez Canal. After some early defeats, they forced the British and Commonwealth troops to retreat. By mid-1941 it looked as if the Germans would soon take control of Egypt.

The war spreads

Germany conquers Russia

As you have read, Hitler and Stalin, leader of the USSR, agreed in 1939 that they would not make war on each other. This was not because they were friends but because it suited them both at the time. Hitler did not stop hating communism and he did not stop wanting extra land for Germany. In June 1941, he broke his agreement with Stalin and invaded the Soviet Union. The Soviet forces were unprepared for the attack. They had to retreat and give up huge areas of their country. By the end of 1941 the Germans had occupied a vast area of the western Soviet Union, including Estonia, Latvia, Lithuania, Byelorussia, Ukraine and Bessarabia.

War in the Far East

War had started in the Far East in 1931, when the Japanese invaded Manchuria (see page 24). Their aim was to get extra land and valuable resources such as oil. They went on to invade the rest of China in 1937.

In 1941 Japanese forces moved to take control of even more of south-east Asia. They invaded French Indo-China and got ready to attack the East Indies and the Philippines.

Only two countries had the power to stop Japan from doing this: Britain and the USA. But before either could act, the Japanese launched surprise attacks on the US navy base at **Pearl Harbor** and

> **i** **Pearl Harbor,** *on the Hawaiian island of Honolulu, was the main base of the US Pacific Fleet. Japanese planes launched from aircraft carriers attacked the base on 7 December 1941. They damaged five battleships and 14 smaller ships, destroyed 120 aircraft and killed 2,400 people.*

SOURCE 7

An American poster of 1942 encourages American soldiers to take revenge on the Japanese for the attack on Pearl Harbor.

SOURCE 6

A small boat rescues a sailor from an American warship set on fire by bombs in the Japanese attack on Pearl Harbor, 7 December 1941.

on British-held Malaya. In the attacks, Britain and the USA lost so many warships that they could not stop the Japanese from carrying out their plans. Source 8 shows the huge area that Japan went on to conquer.

As a result of the attack on Pearl Harbor, the USA declared war on Japan. Germany and Italy, who had become allies of Japan a year earlier, then declared war on the USA. The war which had started in Europe thus spread to the other side of the globe and became a world war.

SOURCE 8

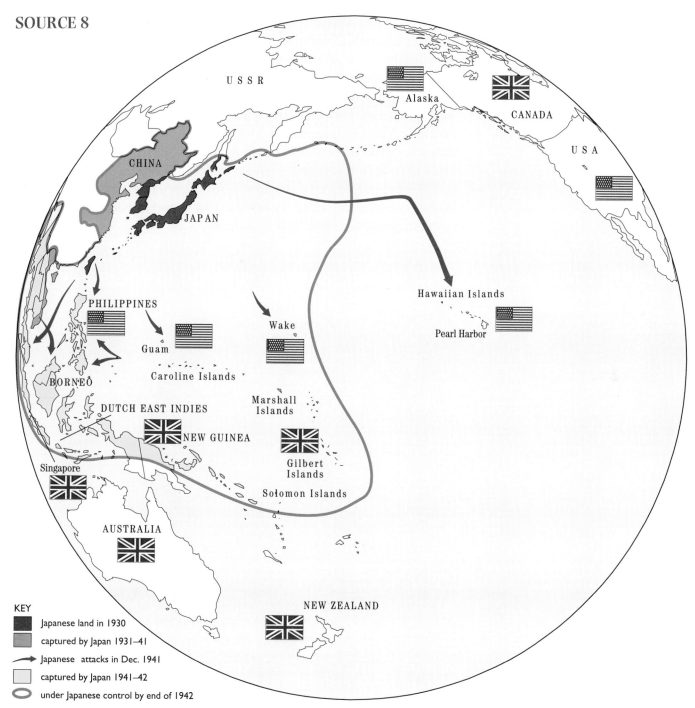

KEY
- Japanese land in 1930
- captured by Japan 1931–41
- Japanese attacks in Dec. 1941
- captured by Japan 1941–42
- under Japanese control by end of 1942

The spread of war in the Far East. This map, which is centred on the Pacific Ocean, shows how the Japanese conquered hundreds of Pacific islands as well as large parts of the Asian mainland.

Global war, 1942–45

activity

Look carefully at source 9, then decide which of these statements is true and which is false.

- Most countries of the world were involved in the Second World War.
- Fighting took place on land, sea and in the air.
- Fighting took place in every continent.
- Most of the fighting took place in Europe.
- The Allied countries outnumbered the Axis countries.

By 1942 the world was divided into two enemy alliances. On one side were Britain, the USA, the USSR and 23 other countries. They were known as The Allies. On the other side were Germany, Italy, Japan and five other countries. They were known as the Axis powers. For the next three years they fought each other in all the areas shown in source 9.

Three important victories in 1942–43 allowed the Allies to start winning back the land they had lost. In the Pacific Ocean the United States navy beat the Japanese navy at the Battle of Midway (June 1942) and started to expel the Japanese from the Pacific islands they had conquered. In Africa the British beat a German army at the Battle of Alamein (November 1942). Then, with the Americans, they drove the Italians and Germans out of North Africa. They went on to invade Italy, forcing it to surrender in July 1943. In the USSR, Soviet forces destroyed a German army after a five-month battle at Stalingrad (August 1942–February 1943) and forced the other German armies in the USSR to retreat.

SOURCE 9

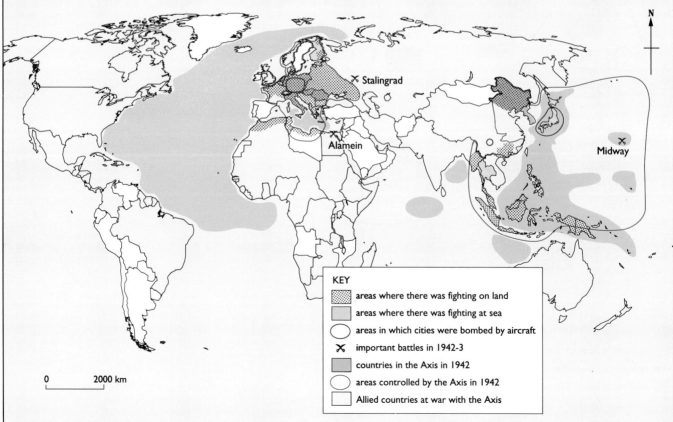

KEY

- areas where there was fighting on land
- areas where there was fighting at sea
- areas in which cities were bombed by aircraft
- X important battles in 1942-3
- countries in the Axis in 1942
- areas controlled by the Axis in 1942
- Allied countries at war with the Axis

Global War, 1942–45.

Defeat of the Axis

By 1944 the Axis armies were retreating in every area of the fighting. Soviet forces pushed the Germans out of the USSR. American and British forces invaded Normandy on 'D-Day' in June 1944 and drove the Germans out of France. In the Pacific, the Americans slowly forced the Japanese to leave the islands they had taken and were soon close enough to Japan to start bombing it from the air. In the Battle of the Atlantic, Allied navy ships destroyed large numbers of German submarines which had been attacking supply boats.

Early in 1945 the Allies closed in on Germany. Soviet forces drove the Germans out of eastern Europe and back into Germany itself.

SOURCE 10

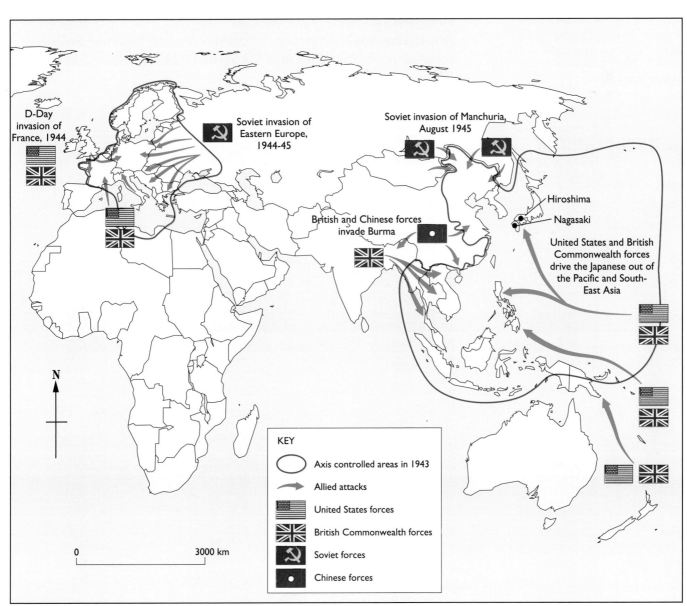

The defeat of the Axis, 1944–45

SOURCE 11

Germany in defeat. A German boy and his mother walk the ruined streets of Berlin in July 1945, looking for somewhere to live.

British and American forces invaded from the west after forcing the Germans out of France, Belgium and the Netherlands. By May 1945 the Russians, British and Americans had control of the whole country. When they entered the capital, Berlin, Hitler committed suicide. A new government surrendered to the Allies a week later.

The war against Japan went on for another fourteen weeks. Japanese soldiers fought with incredible determination to stop the Allies from advancing: the British from Burma, the Americans in the Pacific, the Soviets in Manchuria, and the Chinese in China. It looked as if they would have to invade Japan itself and fight a land war to force the Japanese to surrender. But in August 1945 the United States Air Force dropped two atomic bombs on the cities of Hiroshima and Nagasaki. These recently developed bombs were a thousand times more powerful than any other bomb which then existed. The centres of the two cities were destroyed, 150,000 people were killed and nearly 200,000 were injured. Fearing that the Americans would drop more atomic bombs, the Japanese Emperor surrendered to the Allies on 15 August 1945. The Second World War was over.

assignments

1a Put these events into the order in which they happened.
- Italy's invasion of Greece
- Germany's invasion of Poland
- Japan's attack on the US navy base at Pearl Harbor
- Attack on Egypt by Italian and German forces trying to cut off Britain's oil supplies through the Suez Canal.

b Take each event in turn and explain how it caused the war to spread beyond its starting place in Poland.

2a Put these events into the order in which they happened:
- The Battle of Stalingrad
- The Battle of Midway
- The 'D-Day' invasion of Normandy
- The Battle of Alamein.

b Why were these battles important in changing the course of the war?

3 Imagine that Britain had lost the Battle of Britain in 1940. In as much detail as you can, describe how differently the war might have developed.

5
Men and Women at Arms

About 73 million men and a million women served in the armed forces of 56 countries between 1939 and 1945. Nearly 15 million of them were killed and 25 million wounded. Many who survived felt that their lives had been deeply changed by the experience of war. Part 5 describes the ways in which these people fought and shows how some of them felt about what they were doing.

War on land

Most of the people who fought did so as soldiers, fighting battles on land. In many ways, the soldiers of the Second World War were not very different from those of the First. British, French and German soldiers wore helmets, carried rifles and packs and marched in hobnail boots, just as their fathers and uncles had done in 1914. Source 1 shows how British soldiers were dressed for battle in 1939.

SOURCE 1

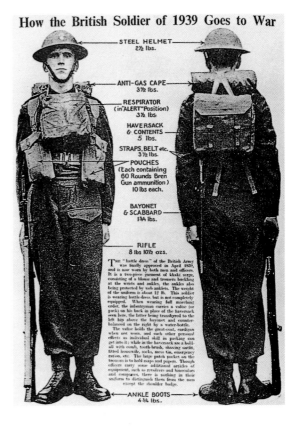

How the British Soldier of 1939 Goes to War

STEEL HELMET
2½ lbs.

ANTI-GAS CAPE
3½ lbs.

RESPIRATOR
(in 'ALERT' Position)
3½ lbs.

HAVERSACK
& CONTENTS
5 lbs.

STRAPS, BELT etc.
3½ lbs.

POUCHES
(Each containing
60 Rounds Bren
Gun ammunition)
10 lbs each.

BAYONET
& SCABBARD
1¾ lbs.

RIFLE
8 lbs 10½ ozs.

ANKLE BOOTS
4¾ lbs.

A picture from a 1939 magazine shows what British soldiers had to take with them into battle.

But there were important differences in the way they fought. The soldiers of 1914–18 spent much of their time sheltering in trenches, occasionally 'going over the top' to attack enemy trenches. Those of 1939–45 spent more time in attack and covered much more ground doing so. This was because every army now used tanks to lead its attacks.

Tanks such as the Panzer (source 2) had terrifying power. Armed with a cannon and heavy machine guns, a tank could destroy almost anything in its way. Source 3 describes what happened when the gunner in a British tank saw German soldiers in a dug-out ahead of him.

SOURCE 2

A Panzer tank crosses the River Bug, dividing Poland from Russia, during the German invasion of the USSR in 1941.

SOURCE 3

Now Stan is ramming a high-explosive shell into the breech. He slaps my leg, signing 'loaded'... A stamp on the button... Then fire, massive, sudden, vivid, brief... But in that brief flame a whirling mass of sandbags, a shattered machine-gun, metal objects, equipment, boxes, helmets, pieces of human bodies, all clear, distinct, in technicolour, quickly dying. Keith comments 'Good shooting!'

Good shooting!... We sit here, within yards of the enemy... press a button and then watch a human being being shredded to death. And cheer. All right, he was a Nazi. All right, it was 'him or us'. All right, we did it under orders. Good shooting! I suppress the desire to ask if any evil thing can be good.

Ken Tout, *Tank! 40 Hours of Battle, August 1944*, 1985

---

i **Tanks** *Gun-carrying armour-plated vehicles moving on tracks. They could travel over rough ground and break through enemy defences to clear a way for soldiers following behind. An attacking army could therefore move faster and further than before. Two famous Second World War tanks were the German Panzer and the American Sherman.*

---

activity

1 How does source 1 help to explain the way the soldiers were marching in source 4?
2 Source 3 tells us what happened when Ken Tout fired at a German dug-out. Does it tell us how he felt about this event? Explain your answer.

i **Jeep**   *Tough four-wheel drive car used for transporting soldiers or equipment, towing guns and other such general purposes – hence its name GP (general purpose) vehicle. Nearly 635,000 were built, making the jeep the most widely used of all Allied combat vehicles.*

i **Flak**   *Short for the German words Flugzeug abwehr kanonen, meaning aircraft attack gun. Allied airmen used the word to describe the fire from these guns – shells which exploded in mid-air into sharp fragments that ripped through aircraft and crew.*

After the tanks came the infantry – the soldiers who marched into battle and fought on foot. Source 4 describes some of the soldiers who marched through Normandy in August 1944, during the Allied invasion of France.

SOURCE 4

One of the things I shall never forget is the sight of the British infantry, plodding steadily up those dusty French roads towards the front, single file, heads bent down against the heavy weight of the kit piled on their backs, armed to the teeth, they were plodding on, slowly and doggedly to the front with the sweat running down their faces and enamel drinking mugs dangling at their hips, never looking back . . . while the **jeeps** *and the lorries and the tanks and all the other traffic went crowding by, smothering them in clouds of dust.*

From a BBC radio news report, August 1944

War in the air

Tanks were only one kind of machine that changed the way battles were fought in the Second World War. Aeroplanes also played a crucial part in the conflict. Aircraft by 1939 were faster and more powerful than those of the First World War. They could fly higher and further, carry heavier loads, and drop larger numbers of bombs.

Flying in bomber aircraft was extremely dangerous. When bombers were over their targets they were likely to be hit by **flak** fired by anti-aircraft guns (Source 6). They could also be attacked by fighter planes.

SOURCE 5

Over the target it was brilliant moonlight, no clouds and I saw Cologne and the Cathedral as plain as anything . . . I got down to twelve thousand [feet] and aimed the bombs and as soon as those bombs hit the ground you've never seen such a change! The colours of searchlights swung up, the guns started out, banging like mad, you could see the tracer coming up and banging round you, all sorts of types. I dived to try and get out of those searchlights, but I was in them for twenty-five minutes! When I got home I had a look at the aircraft – it was shot through with holes! Some as big as a clenched fist! There were a hundred and thirty of them.

Bill Beverley, bomber pilot, interviewed in Edward Smithies, *War in the Air*, 1990

SOURCE 6

THE ATTACK
BEGINS IN THE FACTORY

A poster of 1943 shows an artist's impression of British bombers attacking a city in Germany. The poster was meant to encourage British factories to work hard making aircraft parts, bombs and other materials needed by the Royal Air Force.

Bill Beverley was lucky to get home alive: 47,268 airmen of Britain's Bomber Command were killed on bombing missions between 1940 and 1945. 8,403 were injured. Source 7 describes what happened to just five of them after their plane was attacked by a German fighter aircraft:

SOURCE 7

We were coming back across Holland at about 18,000 feet. The rear gunner called up and said he could see a plane. He was firing at it and meanwhile the plane's fired at us. A lot of the bullets ... went into the . wings ...

I looked out and the whole of the upper surface of the wing was on fire ... I said to the pilot, 'We're on fire. What you gonna do?'
'Bale out!' ...

There's an almighty bang and next minute I'm floating through the air by myself. I just pulled the strap and floated gracefully down to earth! When I landed in the wheat field I broke my leg, broke it there, so I was lucky really. The pilot had his neck broken ... The engineer was killed – he landed but he didn't get a chance to open his parachute. Poor old Joe, the rear gunner, as he baled out he was smothered in petrol and he burned like a torch.

The navigator of a bomber, interviewed in Edward Smithies, *War in the Air*, 1990

SOURCE 8

Members of the Women's Royal Air Force examine photographs of bombing targets taken by aircraft in Germany. Behind them in the Bombing Interpretation Room at RAF Bomber Command, Air Chief Marshal Harris plans the next air raids on Germany.

activity

1 Use sources 5, 6 and 7 to describe the dangers facing airmen in bomber aircraft.
2 The airman in source 7 broke his leg and said later 'I was lucky really.' How can you explain this?
3 Source 6 was an artist's impression of a bombing raid. Judging by sources 5 and 7, was it an accurate impression? Explain your answer.

Fighters

To protect the bombers there were fighter planes. Being a fighter pilot was also extremely dangerous. Travelling at up to 600 kilometres per hour, pilots fought each other with machine guns in the wings or noses of their aircraft. Source 9 describes a few of the dangers. It is what Major Marina Raskova of the Soviet Air Force said to pilots who volunteered to join the all-women regiments which she commanded.

SOURCE 9

The girls I choose must understand beyond any doubt whatsoever that they will be fighting against men, and they must themselves fight like men. If you're chosen you may not be killed – you may be burned so your own mother would not recognise you. You may be blinded. You may lose a hand, a leg. You will lose friends. You may be captured by the Germans. Do you really want to go through with this?
Quoted in Bruce Myles, *Night Witches. The Untold Story of Soviet Women in Combat*, 1981

So what made young women volunteer for such dangerous work? One of the pilots explained her reasons in source 10:

SOURCE 10

I used to fly across our sector and look down at the fields and rivers, and I had this overwhelming feeling that this land was ours and these people [the Germans] were violating [damaging] it, and we must kill them and throw them out.
Quoted in Bruce Myles, *Night Witches*, 1981

Pilots fought for many different reasons. A different motive can be seen in source 11. It was written anonymously by a British fighter pilot whose baby son had recently been killed and his two-year old daughter left with one arm after a German bomb fell on their home. He was describing what happened when he came up behind a German fighter in an air battle in 1943.

SOURCE 11

I could now see the pilot clearly. He was wearing some sort of black leather fur-lined jacket, with his eye goggles pushed back on top of his head. His face turned towards me, but he made no move to leave his seat. I thought he must be wounded and unable to bale out. Such was my blind hate that I actually felt pleased to have this lame duck at my mercy. I . . . lined my sight on the now open cockpit, then thumbed my firing button for the third time. The pilot and his cockpit virtually disappeared in an explosion of cannon shells and ruptured fuel tanks as the aircraft literally fell apart into dozens of pieces . . . All I could feel at that moment was pure joy.
An anonymous pilot, quoted in Chaz Bowyer, *Fighter Pilots of the RAF*, 1984

War at sea

Probably everyone who fought in battle felt fear – fear of being attacked or captured, of being injured and suffering pain, of being mutilated or killed. Sailors who fought at sea were no exception.

The Allied and Axis navies fought each other for control of the shipping routes across the Atlantic, the Mediterranean and the Pacific. These were needed for transporting food, freight, munitions and troops. No country could fight without these things, so whoever got control of the shipping routes would win the war.

The war at sea began in the Atlantic where the German navy attacked Allied ships travelling to Britain and the Soviet Union. Most of these attacks were by submarines which hunted ships unseen beneath the water and blew them up with torpedoes. For protection against submarine attacks, ships travelled in groups called convoys, guarded by armed naval boats such as **destroyers.**

> **i** **Destroyer** *A small, fast warship which hunts submarines and tries to destroy them, usually with* **depth charges.** *These are bombs which they drop into the sea above the submarine's suspected position, and which explode when they reach a pre-set depth.*

Convoys

SOURCE 12

A convoy of ships sailing through the Arctic Ocean towards Murmansk in Russia. An oil tanker had just been hit by a torpedo fired from a U-boat when this picture was taken. Although this convoy was protected by 20 destroyers, only 27 of the 40 ships that started the voyage arrived safely.

Ships were not safe even in convoys. The Germans hunted convoys in 'wolf packs' of up to forty submarines. The destroyers could not protect every ship in a convoy against such massed attacks, and few convoys crossed the Atlantic without losing at least one ship. During the whole of the war, U-boats sank 2,775 British ships – between one and two every single day. Sailing in a convoy was therefore a terrifying experience for many sailors. A Welsh sailor on a Royal Navy destroyer described what it was like on a convoy to Murmansk in Russia. He was then just seventeen years old.

SOURCE 13

On the Murmansk runs there was nothing for us but ceaseless routine and the prospect of death. There never was, in the eight convoys there and back that I witnessed. Apart from the sense of incredulity [disbelief] at being still alive, wondering when our turn would come, there was only the noise and the cold . . . the rough sea and sloshing water on the mess deck, and there was little but wild talk of women and booze and soccer. It was like being in a mobile madhouse. Grown men went steadily and fixedly insane before each other's eyes . . .

Tristan Jones, *Heart of Oak*, 1984

U-boats

There was perhaps only one place more dangerous and frightening than a ship in a convoy, and that was a U-boat. In source 14, a former German submariner described what happened when a British destroyer attacked his U-boat with **depth charges**, forcing it to sit on the sea-bed out of reach of the depth explosions.

SOURCE 14

We sat helpless 265 metres below. Our bodies were stiff from cold, stress and fear. The bilges were flooded with water, oil and urine. Our washrooms were under lock and key; to use them could have resulted in instant death, for the tremendous outside pressure would have acted in reverse. Cans were circulated for the men to relieve themselves. Added to the stench of waste, sweat and oil was the stink of the battery gases. The increasing humidity condensed on the cold steel, dripped from pipes and soaked our clothes. [After 35 hours the British destroyer gave up its attack and went away, and the U-boat surfaced.] Still numb from the murderous assault and stiff from the cold depths, we added up our account. Three U-boats in our group had been sunk. Well over 100 Allied ships had ploughed past us, and we had not been able to sink a single one. We might now expect that some 700,000 tons of war material had safely reached the British Isles. It was not a pretty picture.

Herbert A. Werner, *Iron Coffins*, 1969

activity

1 Look at sources 12–14.
a Why was it so dangerous for ships to be at sea during the Second World War?
b As it was so dangerous for ships to be at sea, why didn't they simply stay in port until the war was over?
2 In sources 13 and 14 sailors on opposite sides in the war described their experiences. How were their experiences
a similar,
b different?
3a What impression does source 15 give of U-boats?
b How does this differ from the impression created by source 14?
c Which of sources 14 and 15 do you think is more useful as evidence of U-boat warfare in the Second World War? Explain your answer.

SOURCE 15

A propaganda photograph taken in 1943 shows German U-boats on a training exercise in the Baltic Sea.

Combined operations

activity

Look at source 16. Why was it necessary for the army, the navy and the air force to join together in a combined operation to invade Normandy?

Many Second World War battles were fought by combined forces of soldiers, sailors and airmen. This happened most often when the Allied forces had to cross the sea to attack Axis armies. Combined Allied forces were used, for example, to invade North Africa in 1942, Italy in 1943 and France in 1944 (see pages 44–45). On such occasions, naval ships transported and landed whole armies of soldiers on enemy coasts, while air force planes protected them from enemy air attack and bombed enemy positions.

Source 16 shows part of the biggest combined operation of the war: the Allied 'D-Day' landings in Normandy. Four thousand ships took 185,000 soldiers and 20,000 vehicles across the Channel to invade German-occupied France. This invasion force was protected by over a thousand warships and by thousands of aircraft. Before the landings began, bomber aircraft bombed German defences, and 20,000 airborne troops were dropped by parachute to seal off the invasion area by capturing bridges and important roads. Allied losses in the invasion were 2,500 soldiers killed and 8,500 injured.

SOURCE 16

This photograph, taken on 6 June 1944, shows part of one of the invasion beaches in Normandy after its capture by Allied forces on D-Day. The barrage balloons floating above the ships were put there to stop German fighter planes attacking them while they unloaded.

SOURCE 17

A British commando unit attacks a German gun site in Normandy after landing in France on D-day in 1944.

Special forces

Up to 1939 wars were usually fought in pitched battles between large armies or navies. The Second World War was different. Fighting was also done by a great variety of small, specialised armed forces.

The first special forces created in the Second World War were called commandos. With around 500 soldiers, a commando unit was much smaller than a normal army unit. The job of a commando was to make sudden surprise raids on the coasts of occupied countries such as France or Greece. What made commandos different was that they fought without the support of big guns, tanks, or other heavy weapons. Instead they used small arms and unarmed combat techniques when fighting (source 17).

Kamikaze

Commando raids were dangerous, but the risks that commandos ran were small compared to those run by 'special attack' units in the Japanese, German, Italian and British armed forces. Servicemen in these units volunteered for missions they knew would almost certainly result in their deaths. They used such things as human torpedoes, hand-held bombs and explosive boats and planes to make suicidal attacks on enemies. The best known were the **Kamikaze** pilots of the Japanese air force.

Kamikaze pilots flew planes filled with high explosive and just enough fuel to get to their targets, which were Allied warships in the Pacific Ocean. When a pilot found an Allied ship he dived onto it, giving up his life for the certainty of a direct hit. Why did pilots volunteer to do this? One reason can be seen in source 18. It is taken from the memoirs of a *kamikaze* pilot who survived the war because bad weather caused the cancellation of his flight. It describes the moment when his commander told him he had been chosen to die. The commander said:

SOURCE 18

As you know, the army is short of pilots, petrol, planes and ammunition – in fact, everything. We find ourselves at a dead-end. There is just one last resort left to us: to crash onto the decks of enemy aircraft carriers, as your comrades have done before you. Two hours ago, our squadron received the order to form a Special Attack Corps. I am compelled to ask you to . . . to . . . undertake this mission.

R. Nagatsuka, *I Was a Kamikaze*, 1973

> ℹ️ **Kamikaze** *is one way of pronouncing a Japanese word which means 'divine wind'. The wind was a typhoon that destroyed a fleet of ships trying to invade Japan hundreds of years ago, so the word was used to describe the pilots who tried to destroy the American invasion fleet with suicide attacks in 1944–45. However, Japanese people rarely pronounced the word in this way. They pronounced it as* shimpu. *The pilots belonged to units known as* Shimpu Tokubetsu Kogekitai, *meaning Divine Wind Special Attack Force.*

SOURCE 19

This photograph shows the final second of a *kamikaze* attack on the battleship USS Missouri on 11 April 1945. A moment later the plane hit the ship and exploded. It looks as if the plane was going to hit the men in the gun turret but it actually struck the side of the ship and did little damage.

But what did the pilots feel about being chosen for suicide attacks? According to one of their commanders, speaking after the war was over:

SOURCE 20

We did not consider our attacks to be suicide. The pilot did not start out on his mission with the intention of committing suicide . . . in a spirit of despair. He looked upon himself as a human bomb which would destroy a certain part of the enemy fleet . . . and died happy in the conviction that his death was a step towards the final victory.

Lt General Torashiro Kawabe, interrogated soon after the war by the United States Strategic Bombing Survey

In the last months of the war suicide volunteers also attacked Allied ships with exploding boats. In all, around 5,000 volunteers were killed in air and sea *kamikaze* attacks. They sank four major Allied warships and 31 smaller warships such as destroyers. But although they damaged nearly three hundred other ships in their attacks, many of these were quickly repaired and brought back into action.

activity

1 According to source 18, why did the Japanese make *kamikaze* attacks on Allied ships?

2a How many Japanese died in *kamikaze* attacks? How many ships did they sink?

b Judging by source 20, would men have volunteered for *kamikaze* attacks if they had known the answer to question 2a?

3 The United States government did not allow the American press to print photographs like source 19. Why do you think this was?

The underground war

> **i** **The Resistance** *Secret organisations in conquered countries which carried out surprise attacks and sabotage against the occupying forces. Resisters in France were known as the Maquis. In other countries, they were 'the Underground' or 'the Secret Army'. Both women and men were active fighters in the Resistance.*

> **i** **Partisans** *Armed fighters who not only mounted acts of resistance and sabotage but also carried out guerilla warfare against occupying forces.*

Several million fighters of the Second World War did not belong to any of the armed forces but to **resistance** groups.

There were resistance groups in every occupied country. Their aim was to make life difficult for the occupiers in any way they could. Mostly they used sabotage to do this. They blew up railways, cut power cables and set fire to buildings. Resisters also used sabotage at work. Railway workers, for example, sent trains to the wrong places. Factory workers deliberately made faulty goods. Source 21 shows some of the acts of sabotage of the Polish resistance.

SOURCE 21

Locomotives damaged	*6,930*
Transports derailed	*732*
Railway wagons damaged	*19,058*
Military vehicles damaged	*4,326*
Railway bridges blown up	*38*
Military warehouses burnt	*122*
Defective parts for aircraft engines produced	*4,710*
Defective artillery shells produced	*92,000*
Attacks on Germans	*5,733*

Stefan Korbonski, *The Polish Underground State, 1939–45*, 1978

In south-east Europe and the USSR, the resistance fighters were called **partisans**. In Yugoslavia alone around a million men and women belonged to partisan groups.

The Germans did not regard partisans and resistance fighters as soldiers and so did not treat them as prisoners of war when they captured them. Captured fighters were usually executed without a trial. Many were tortured to make them give information about their comrades (Source 24).

Why did so many people become resisters when they knew they faced torture and death if caught? One reason can be seen in source 22. It is an interview, lasting less than a minute, in which a French woman talked to British historian, Roderick Kedward.

SOURCE 22

I . . . have only one thing to say. I came home from shopping on 9 June 1944 to find my husband and son hanging from the balcony of our house. They were just two of a hundred men seized at random and killed in cold blood by the SS. The children and the wives were forced to watch while they strung them up to the lamp-posts and balconies outside their own homes. What else is there for me to say?

Roderick Kedward, *Resistance in Vichy France*, 1978

---

activity

4 Select any three acts of sabotage from source 21 and explain what you think the Polish resistance was hoping to achieve through them.
5 The interview in source 22 is all the woman would tell the interviewer. It ends with her asking, 'What more is there for me to say?' Is there anything that the interview does not tell you about why she became a resister? What questions might you ask to find out about this?

In the Soviet Union, partisans had to swear an oath when they joined the movement. This oath helps to explain their aims.

SOURCE 23

I swear to work a terrible, merciless and unrelenting revenge upon the enemy for the burning of our cities and villages, for the murder of our children, and for the torture and atrocities committed against our people. Blood for blood! Death for death!

John A. Armstrong, *Soviet Partisans in World War II*, 1964

SOURCE 24

This poster shows ten French Resistance fighters executed in February 1944 for sabotage and killing. Put up all over France by the Germans, the poster says 'Freedom fighters? Liberation by an army of criminals!' The details under each man's portrait tell us that they were all foreigners and that seven were Jewish. The pictures beneath show some of their 'crimes' – blowing up railway lines and shooting German soldiers.

activity

1 What does source 23 tell you about why Russian men and women became partisans?

2 Look at source 24. Why do you think the Germans put up this poster all over France?

The intelligence war

> **i** **Intelligence** *Information about an enemy's plans or actions. Such information was gained by spying, questioning enemy prisoners, and by intercepting enemy messages.*

Many servicemen and servicewomen did vital war work without fighting. They were involved in the gathering and processing of **intelligence**.

The most important intelligence work was deciphering the secret codes that enemies used when sending radio messages. The hardest codes to break were those used by the German armed forces. They coded important radio signals with a machine called *Enigma*.

SOURCE 25

A German general watches his signals staff using an Enigma machine to encode radio messages during the German invasion of France in 1940.

i **Wrens** *Members of the WRNS – the Women's Royal Naval Service. They worked as mechanics, drivers, despatch riders, radio and radar operators, and in many other non-combat naval jobs. The Wrens of HMS Pembroke V (P5 for short) mostly did intelligence work.*

activity

1 Suggest why this army division used the Enigma coding machine to send this report.

2 What uses could the Allies have made of this report?

The Enigma machine had a typewriter keyboard linked to three wheels which could be rotated through 26 positions each. The wheels and keyboard together could produce 200 million million million different combinations of letters. This made a code that was almost impossible to break.

In Britain, the job of breaking the Enigma codes was done by a group of brilliant scientists and mathematicians at Bletchley Park. To help them decipher messages they devised a machine called a 'bombe' which tested coded signals on a panel of rotating drums.

Two thousand **Wrens** of the Royal Navy operated the bombes. It could take anything from fifteen minutes to fifteen hours to try all the positions for one message. The information that they decoded was given the very highest security classification: ultra top secret. Source 28 shows the kind of message that might come out at the end of the process. It is an incomplete report on the strength of a German army division in June 1944, shortly before the Allied D-Day landings in Normandy. The first figure shows how many of each item the division had. The last shows any shortage of each item. The meaning of the other figures was unknown.

SOURCE 26

Report of state of 42 Jaeger Division

II	Personnel	Men 10855, nil
III	Material	Pistols 2734, nil
		Rifles 11 773, nil
		MP (sub-machine guns) 428, 580, 40, nil
		LMG (light machine guns) 511, nil
		Mortars 104, nil
		LIG 13, 2
		SIG nil 4, 4, nil
		LFH 9, nil
		SFH 7, 1, 1, nil
		Heavy A/T guns 22, nil
IV	State of training	Varies. Some elements still lack basic training and weapon and firing training . . .
V	Special difficulties	Serious deficiency of motor transport makes difficult supply and supervision of troops employed over wide area . . .
VI	Operational readiness	Conditionally ready for defence.

Peter Calvocoressi, *Top Secret Ultra*, 1980

assignments

I Look carefully at source 27 on this page and overleaf.

a Describe the impression that the artist creates of fighting in the Second World War.

b Judging by what you have read in Part 5 about fighting in the Second World War, do you think it is an accurate impression? Explain your answer.

c Consider what sources the artist might have used to draw this comic strip.

(i) Choose three sources from this chapter which give a very different impression from that created by the comic.

(ii) Say what picture of war is created by the three sources you have chosen.

d How convincing do you find source 27 as a picture of fighting in the Second World War? Explain your answer fully.

SOURCE 27

A war story which appeared in 'Victor', a British childrens comic, in 1976.

assignments

SOURCE 27 (continued)

2 The sources in Part 5 were chosen to show what it was like to be on active service in the Second World War. The sources include:

- memoirs written by people who took part
- interviews with people who took part
- photographs
- paintings.

a Find two examples of each kind of source.

b Which kind of source have you found most useful for finding out (i) what fighting in the war was like, (ii) what people felt about fighting in the war?

c Put each pair of sources you have chosen into an order of usefulness, with the most useful at the top. Explain why you think they are more useful than the others.

d No source of evidence is ever completely reliable or entirely useful. Is there anything about the sources at the top of your list which affects their reliability or usefulness?

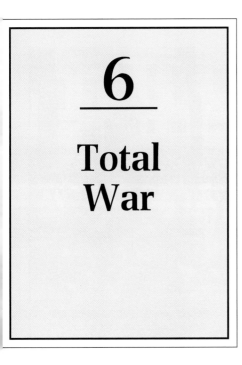

6

Total War

The Second World War was a total war. This means that it was not fought only on battlefields by armed forces. Civilians were also directly involved. For example, millions of townspeople risked being killed, injured or made homeless by bombs dropped from the air. In every country, civilians were involved in making weapons and other war materials. And in defeated countries civilians had to live under the rule of enemy occupying forces who treated them harshly.

How did occupation affect people's lives?

The Germans and the Japanese occupied each of the countries they conquered. This meant that 770 million people in 30 countries came under enemy occupation (see source 2 on page 39 and source 8 on page 43).

Occupation involved three things. First, the occupiers imposed their laws and government on the people. Second, they kept large armies there to prevent rebellions against their rule. Third, they plundered the countries of materials, food and machinery. These aspects of occupation can be seen in sources 1 and 2.

SOURCE 1

Directive for military government in England

1 *The main task of military government is to make full use of the country's resources for the needs of fighting troops and the requirements of the German war economy.*

2 *An essential condition for securing the labour of the country is that law and order should prevail. Law and order will therefore be established...*

3 *Armed rebels of either sex will be treated with the utmost severity...*

4 *The able-bodied male population between the ages of 17 and 45 will be interned [imprisoned] and dispatched to the Continent with the minimum of delay...*

From an order that the Germans intended to issue after invading Britain in 1940

activity

1 Look at source 1. If the Germans had occupied Britain in 1940, what would have happened to
a men aged 17 to 45, and
b armed rebels?

The only part of the United Kingdom occupied by Germany during the war was the Channel Islands. This photograph shows a German army band playing in St Helier on the island of Jersey.

Every occupied country had to pay the costs of maintaining the army that occupied it. France, for example, had to pay 400 million francs every day. The more an occupying army took from a country, the less there was for its people. Source 3 describes the shortages created by the German plunder of Czechoslovakia. It was written by a Czech in an anonymous letter to a friend in Britain.

SOURCE 3

Foreign occupation changes every detail of your life . . . You cannot get proper food. It is not the rationing itself which brings discomfort but rather the way your food is rationed and why. You know that your country was rich a short time ago and you've seen it plundered. Your restriction is not a necessary sacrifice which you are making for your country, your army, your struggle. You are starving in order that the men you hate should be well fed . . . Your mother or your wife must stand with their food cards in long queues before the shops; they must stand for hours supervised by the German police. You are cold at home because you cannot get any coal. You cannot get your socks darned because there is no wool or cotton. You cannot wash your hands because there is no soap.

Shiela Grant Duff, *A German Protectorate. The Czechs under Nazi Rule*, 1970

activity

1a What impression does source 2 create of the German occupation of the Channel Islands?
b Do you think the photographer was friendly or hostile towards the Germans? Explain your answer.

Resistance and repression

In every country which the Germans and Japanese occupied, people resisted their rule. The simplest way of doing this was by refusing to cooperate with them. For example, many French people pretended

i **Gestapo**   Short for
Geheime Staatspolizei, the
secret state police in Nazi
Germany. The Gestapo had the
power to arrest people without
warrant, to imprison them
without trial, and to torture and
kill them. As a result they were
the most hated and feared
organisation in Nazi-occupied
Europe. The **Kenpeitai**, the
Japanese military police, had
similar powers and were equally
hated and feared.

not to understand orders given in German. Dutch people got up and left when German soldiers entered their cafés. Indonesians avoided saluting the Japanese flag. More dangerously, several million men and women took part in armed resistance. They became partisans and used sabotage and murder against the occupiers.

Both the Germans and Japanese dealt harshly with resisters. In German-held countries this was done by the **Gestapo**. Source 4 describes one of their methods of dealing with resistance. It is a poster put up on walls in the French city of Nantes in 1941.

SOURCE 4

Cowardly criminals in the pay of England and Moscow have killed, by shooting in the back, the Feldkommandant (Field Commander) of Nantes on the morning of October 20, 1941. To date the murderers have not been caught.

In payment for this crime I have already ordered that fifty hostages be shot.

Given the seriousness of the crime, fifty more hostages will be shot if the guilty parties are not arrested by midnight, October 23.

I offer a reward totalling 15 million francs to those citizens who contribute towards the discovery of the guilty parties.

Milton Dank, *The French against the French: Collaboration and Resistance*, 1974

On that particular occasion, nobody gave information about the murders, and the hostages were all shot. Similar events took place all over occupied Europe (source 5).

SOURCE 5

A German soldier shoots Yugoslavs who have been accused of resistance activities.

activity

2 Look at source 3.
a The person who wrote this letter describes three ways in which occupation made daily life uncomfortable. What were they?
b The writer was not complaining only about physical discomfort. What was his main complaint?
3 Read source 4.
a What is a hostage?
b Suppose that somebody who witnessed the shooting of the German commander read this poster. Why might he or she want to tell the German police about it?
c Suggest why nobody did give information despite what this poster said.

Jeanne d'Arc *was a French peasant girl who, from childhood, believed she heard the voices of saints telling her to free France from English invaders during the Hundred Years' War. She became so famous as a result of hearing these voices that the French King Charles VII gave her military training and put her in charge of an army. Jeanne drove the English out of the city of Orléans which they were besieging and went on to win many battles against them. In 1430 she was captured in a battle and tried by the English as a witch. They burned her to death in Rouen in 1431.*

Why did people collaborate with the enemy?

Many people did not dare resist. They simply got on with their lives as best they could. Some went further and helped the occupiers. Many mayors, police and other local officials helped them keep law and order. Armed bands of local volunteers helped them fight partisans. Local merchants, traders and bankers did business with them. Young women went out with soldiers. Such people were known as collaborators.

People collaborated with the occupiers for many reasons. Sources 6–8 help us to understand one set of reasons. Source 6 is from a poster which French collaborators put up in 1944 on the anniversary of the death of **Jeanne d'Arc**.

SOURCE 6

1412	Jeanne is born at Donremy
1429	Jeanne defeats the English at Orléans
1430	Jeanne is taken prisoner at Compiègne
1431	Jeanne is burnt alive at Rouen, BY THE ENGLISH.
1939	France is dragged into the war BY THE ENGLISH.
1940	France is betrayed at Dunkirk ... BY THE ENGLISH.
1942	France is stripped of its colonies BY THE ENGLISH.
1943	French towns are bombed every day BY THE ENGLISH.

Yesterday like today, A SINGLE ENEMY, the English ...

Pascal Ory, *La France Allemande (German France)*, 1977

Source 7 is part of a letter written by a former collaborator to a French historian researching the history of occupied France in the 1970s.

SOURCE 7

I was a 'collabo'. I was sixteen years old in 1940 ... We had been defeated. What a sorry sight it was to see the troops marching miserably back without having really fought, thinking only of saving their skin, without dignity, without pride ... On the other side, young, handsome, healthy-looking athletes who conducted themselves as brave and loyal soldiers ... Opponents to respect, why should they not tomorrow be allies, friends, and put an end for ever to the fatal hatred between French and Germans? ... And then why should we not rebuild Europe on different foundations?

Henri Amouroux, *La Grande Histoire des Français sous l'Occupation*, vol. 3, 1978

A well-known collaborator, the writer Pierre Drieu la Rochelle, had similar reasons for collaborating. They are seen in a note (source 8) he wrote shortly before committing suicide in 1945, after the Germans had been driven out of France. The note was a statement addressed to the French Resistance movement.

activity

1 Look at source 6.
a Which side was France on when the war began in 1939?
b What point do you think the collaborators were trying to make with this poster?
c How does it help explain why they collaborated with the Germans?
2 What reasons for collaboration can be seen in source 7?
3 What similar reason can be seen in source 8?

Look at source 9.
4 Describe as accurately as you can what was happening in this scene.
5 The woman carrying her baby was being abused, yet many people around her, including a policeman, were laughing. How can this be explained?
6 The woman on the platform was smiling. Do you think she thought that what was happening to her was funny? Explain your answer.

SOURCE 8

Yes, I am a traitor. Yes, I have been on good terms with the enemy. I have given French secrets to the enemy. It's not my fault that the enemy hasn't been clever ...

Yes, I'm not an ordinary patriot, a narrow nationalist: I am an internationalist. I'm not only a Frenchman, I'm a European.

You are too, without meaning to be and without knowing it. But we have played our cards and I have lost. I ask for death.

Pierre Drieu la Rochelle, *Exorde (Introduction)*, published posthumously in 1961

Understandably, resisters hated collaborators. When the war ended in 1945, they took revenge. In France they secretly executed around 30,000 collaborators without trials. In scenes like the one photographed in source 9, thousands of women had their heads shaved bare for being 'horizontal collaborators' – meaning that they had had sexual relations with German soldiers.

SOURCE 9

After their liberation from German rule in 1944, the people of this town near Paris punish a 'horizontal collaborator' by shaving off her hair in public and driving her out of town.

Displaced people

> **i** **Refugees** *are people who flee their homes to live elsewhere, usually in another country, in order to escape danger or to avoid persecution. In recent years, for example, thousands of refugees have fled from Bosnia to Austria to escape the civil war there.*

Refugees

Having a home is one of the basic needs of all human beings, and being homeless is a disaster for anyone. Many millions of people suffered that disaster in the Second World War.

In every country where there was fighting, terrified people left their homes to seek refuge in safer places. In Japan, for example, ten million people left their homes in the cities to escape American bombs, and went to live in the countryside. In Yugoslavia, where the Germans ruled with great savagery (source 5), hundreds of thousands of people were constantly on the move to escape capture.

The biggest movement of refugees took place at the end of the war in 1945. Sixteen million Germans lived in the occupied countries of eastern Europe. As the Soviet army advanced across Europe (see page 45) many of them fled in panic, terrified by thoughts of what the Soviet troops would do to them. Those who did not flee were rounded up and transported in appalling conditions to Germany. Out of 16 million German refugees in 1945, around 3 million died of cold, hunger, disease and exhaustion.

SOURCE 10

German refugees cross the River Elbe in 1945 to escape from the Soviet army advancing from the east.

Deportation

Millions of people in the defeated countries were taken from their homes to work for the occupying forces. Over a million Koreans and Chinese were sent to Japan to work on farms and in mines and factories. Many thousands of Korean women were forced to be prostitutes for Japanese soldiers. In occupied Europe 3.5 million people, mostly Russians and Poles, were sent to Germany to do slave labour. Source 11 gives us an idea of the life these people led.

SOURCE 11

1 *Polish farmworkers no longer have the right to complain.*

2 *Polish farmworkers may not leave the localities in which they are employed and have a curfew from 1 October to 31 March from 2000 hours to 0600 hours, and from 1 April to 30 September from 2100 hours to 0500 hours.*

3 *The use of bicycles is strictly prohibited . . .*

4 *Visiting churches, regardless of faith, is strictly prohibited.*

5 *Visits to theatres, cinemas or other cultural entertainment are strictly prohibited.*

6 *Visiting restaurants is strictly prohibited.*

7 *Sexual intercourse with women and girls is strictly prohibited . . .*

8 *Gatherings of Polish farmworkers after work are prohibited . . .*

9 *The use of railways, buses, or other public conveyances is strictly prohibited . . .*

10 *Polish farmworkers have to work daily for as long as is demanded by the employer . . .*

11 *Every employer has the right to beat Polish farmworkers.*

A government order telling German farmers how to treat Polish farmworkers in 1943

It wasn't only in the occupied countries that people were expelled from their homes. In the Allied countries, people with foreign backgrounds were put in prison camps so that they could not help the enemy in an invasion. In the USA, for example, residents and citizens of Japanese and Far Eastern origin were kept in camps until the end of the war. Most expulsions took place in the USSR where the Government did not trust the non-Russian peoples to stay loyal. It sent 400,000 German-speaking people from the Volga region to prison camps in distant Siberia and deported a million non-Russians from around the Black Sea to Central Asia.

The most horrifying deportations were carried out by the Germans. In all the countries under their control, the Germans arrested and imprisoned every Jewish person they could find. Their aim was to destroy the entire Jewish race. To kill the estimated 11 million Jews living in Europe, they set up 'extermination camps' in remote areas of Poland. Long trains of goods wagons transported the captured Jews to the camps, where they were murdered. Part 8 of this book will tell you in detail how and why this happened.

activity

1 Look at source 11.

a People in most countries have certain basic rights and freedoms – for example, the right to follow their religion or the right of free speech. What rights were taken away from Poles by this government order?

b Suggest why the Germans deprived Polish workers in Germany of so many rights and freedoms.

Shortages and rationing

Every time a submarine sank a supply ship, or every time a plane bombed a factory, it destroyed part of the enemy's trade and industry. In every country at war, it was not long before this led to shortages of food, fuel, clothing and many other necessities.

Most countries introduced rationing to cope with shortages. This meant that people could only buy limited amounts of the things in short supply. In Britain they were issued with ration books like the one shown in source 12. These contained a separate page for each rationed item, divided into squares that were cancelled each week. In Germany they had ration cards and in Japan books of tickets. Source 12 shows the food rations people could buy in two countries in 1941.

SOURCE 12

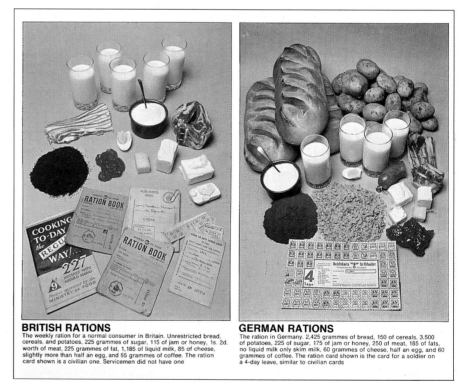

BRITISH RATIONS
The weekly ration for a normal consumer in Britain. Unrestricted bread, cereals, and potatoes, 225 grammes of sugar, 115 of jam or honey, 1s. 2d. worth of meat, 225 grammes of fat, 1,185 of liquid milk, 85 of cheese, slightly more than half an egg, and 55 grammes of coffee. The ration card shown is a civilian one. Servicemen did not have one

GERMAN RATIONS
The ration in Germany. 2,425 grammes of bread, 150 of cereals, 3,500 of potatoes, 225 of sugar, 175 of jam or honey, 250 of meat, 185 of fats, no liquid milk only skim milk, 60 grammes of cheese, half an egg, and 60 grammes of coffee. The ration card shown is the card for a soldier on a 4-day leave, similar to civilian cards

Rations and ration cards.

So many goods were so strictly rationed that people tried all sorts of substitutes for them. British people ate such things as carrot marmalade, powdered eggs, spam and 'Woolton pie' made from potatoes, turnips and cauliflower. The Japanese ate sausages made from seal meat, wore clogs when their shoes wore out and smoked cigarettes made from aubergine leaves. Germans drank coffee made from roasted acorns and wore clothes made from wood pulp.

activity

1 Look at source 12. Which country had the most generous rations in 1941?
2 Work in a group of four.
a Two of you are going to set up a stall in a market like the one in source 13, where you will try to swap some of your possessions for rationed goods. What possessions will you put on display? What makes you think anyone will be interested in them?
b The other two have rationed goods that they do not need (for example, non-smokers do not need their tobacco ration). What unneeded items will you take to the market for exchange? Which possessions on display are you interested in, if any? What are you prepared to give for them?

SOURCE 13

Ukrainians in the city of Kharkov in 1942 offer their valuables in exchange for rationed food, cigarettes and other goods in short supply. List all the things you can see that the people were trying to exchange.

People everywhere grew tired of rationing. Everybody wanted more than their share. This led to the creation of 'black markets' in which people secretly paid high prices for goods such as meat, clothing, cigarettes, sweets, petrol or soap. People also tried to get more than their ration by swapping their valuables for rationed goods. Source 13 shows this happening in the Ukraine in 1942.

People may have disliked rationing, but in most countries it made sure that nobody starved. In a few countries, however, rationing could not prevent this. Holland, for example, had been so badly plundered by the Germans that the weekly rations in late 1944 were 3 pounds of bread, 4 pounds of potatoes, a slice of cheese and a few vegetables. There was no milk, sugar, meat or fat. But worse was to come. That winter was the worst in living memory. The rations fell to two slices of bread a day, a few potatoes and rotten vegetables, but no fuel to cook them with. Twenty thousand people died of starvation in the Dutch 'hunger winter' of 1944–45.

Thought control

Propaganda

In every country at war governments did all they could to make sure that people supported the war. This meant trying to control the way they thought about it, mainly by using propaganda.

Propaganda is a form of advertising. Its aim is to persuade large numbers of people to believe certain things, usually to do with politics. Propaganda can be done visually, using film, television or posters; it can be printed in newspapers, magazines, leaflets; and it can be spoken, in radio broadcasts or speeches, for example.

One of the commonest forms of propaganda during the war was the wall poster. Cheap to produce, colourful and eye-catching, posters like sources 14–16 put across messages simply and quickly.

SOURCE 14

This Soviet Russian poster appeared soon after the Germans invaded the USSR in 1941. It says 'Your Mother Country Needs You!' The woman who represents Russia is holding a soldier's oath of loyalty in her hand.

SOURCE 15

An American poster of 1942 shows a weeping child and his dead parents in the wreckage of their home, with the face of Hitler sneering in the background.

SOURCE 16

A British poster of 1942 shows a shepherd and his dogs bringing in sheep on the South Downs in England.

Very few people had television at the time of the Second World War but most had a radio. This meant that each country could transmit its propaganda directly into the homes of people in enemy countries. German radio, for example, transmitted a daily programme in which a British traitor, William Joyce (known as Lord Haw Haw) tried to undermine British people's confidence by giving them bad or misleading news. Britain in turn transmitted programmes to occupied countries and to Germany. By 1945 the BBC was using 137 transmitters to broadcast in 47 languages.

Censorship

Another method of controlling what people thought was censorship. In every country, government officials called censors checked written and printed materials, films and photographs to make sure they did not contain anything that might help the enemy or damage their country's war effort. When censors found such material they either removed or banned it. In Britain, for example, a Censorship Bureau banned all press photographs which showed discouraging scenes such as dead air-raid victims, wounded soldiers or houses destroyed by bombs.

In some countries, censorship was very strict. In Japan the government closed down thousands of newspapers and magazines and controlled all news through a single news agency. Film scripts were censored before shooting began and the films censored before they were screened. In ways like these, the government ensured that Japanese people never got to know what was happening in the war. As Prime Minister Tojo of Japan put it, 'The masses are foolish. If we tell them the facts, morale will collapse.'

activity

1 Work in a group of three. Each choose one of the posters on these pages and prepare a one-minute talk in which you tell the others:
a what you think the poster was trying to persuade people to think or to do, and
b what methods the artist used to achieve this.
2 Look through the photographs in Parts 5 and 6 of this book, and choose one you think a government might have censored. Explain your choice.

Economies at war

| i | *We use the word* **economy** *to describe everything in a country that is concerned with making, buying and selling things. A country's industry, agriculture, trade, banking and commerce are therefore all part of its economy. A country with a strong economy produces a great deal, sells to other countries more that it buys from them, and provides its people with a good standard of living.* |

Wars use up and destroy huge amounts of material and equipment. A bomb cannot be remade once it has exploded. A crashed plane cannot be rebuilt. A sunken ship stays at the bottom of the sea. Yet while the war goes on, all these things must be replaced if the armies are to continue fighting.

Between 1939 and 1945, therefore, vast quantities of metal, chemicals, rubber, glass and hundreds of other materials were constantly being destroyed and replaced. Victory didn't depend only on which side had the strongest armies. It depended also on which side could produce enough weapons, ammunition and equipment to keep the armies going, and that depended on which had the strongest **economy**.

The American economy

The country with the strongest economy was the United States of America. This may seem surprising. When the war began millions of Americans were out of work and the country was in an economic depression (see page 17). But as soon as the US government started buying weapons and war equipment, millions found work in the factories that made them. The USA also had huge supplies of raw materials and energy, and was soon providing war material for its allies, especially Britain and the USSR.

SOURCE 17

Workers assemble the nose turrets of bomber aircraft at the Douglas Aircraft factory in Long Beach, California, in 1943.

Between 1940 and 1945 American factories produced more than 300,000 war planes, 96,000 tanks, 61,000 heavy guns, seven million rifles, two million lorries and half a million jeeps, as well as all the other things soldiers needed for warfare: uniforms, boots, food, medicines, radios and a hundred other things. This put money into the pockets of the workers who made them, and it made their companies rich.

SOURCE18

How an American B-29 'Superfortress' bomber was constructed. The B-29 was the largest bomber made during the Second World War.

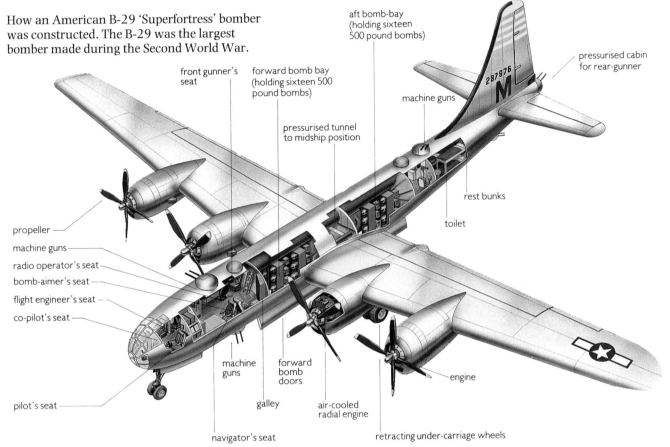

- aft bomb-bay (holding sixteen 500 pound bombs)
- pressurised cabin for rear-gunner
- front gunner's seat
- forward bomb bay (holding sixteen 500 pound bombs)
- machine guns
- pressurised tunnel to midship position
- rest bunks
- toilet
- propeller
- machine guns
- radio operator's seat
- bomb-aimer's seat
- flight engineer's seat
- co-pilot's seat
- machine guns
- forward bomb doors
- engine
- pilot's seat
- galley
- air-cooled radial engine
- retracting under-carriage wheels
- navigator's seat

activity

Make a table like the one here, then look carefully at source 18. In the first column of your table, write down at least six important parts of the aircraft, for example wings, or wheels, or pilot's controls. In the second, list the materials that are needed to make each thing. In the third, show what kinds of worker were likely to be needed for the production of a bomber aircraft. For example:

Aircraft parts	Materials used to make each part	Workers needed to provide these materials
pilot's controls	wiring switches dials	electricians
	radio	radio engineers

activity

1 How does source 19 help to explain General Zhukov's comment in source 21 that the evacuation of the factories was 'a heroic feat'?
2 Why do you think Zhukov thought that feats such as the one described in source 19 were just as important as 'the greatest battles of the war'?

The Soviet economy

The Soviet Union was almost defeated when the Germans invaded in 1941 (see page 45). One reason why it survived was that the Soviets moved their biggest factories out of reach of the Germans. They took the machines and buildings of 1,523 factories to pieces and transported them in over a million train-loads to new sites in the east of the country. This was hard on many Soviet people. Millions of workers were forced to move with their factories far from home. Hours of work increased and conditions of work could be awful, as source 19 shows. It describes how workers from the Ukraine rebuilt their steel plant in the Ural mountains.

SOURCE 19

They were given seventy-five days, from the end of December 1941 to mid-March 1942. They had to re-establish seven main and eleven auxiliary production shops together with railway lines, water supplies, air shafts; all this in 45 degrees of frost, with the soil frozen to a depth of two metres. They had to heat the ground, drill it and break it up with explosives, keep the concrete from freezing, working round the clock, often holding production conferences at 2 and 3 a.m. The job was finished ahead of schedule, in six weeks.

John Barber and Mark Harrisson, *The Soviet Home Front 1941–1945*, 1991

SOURCE 20

Inside a tank factory in the Ural Mountains of the Soviet Union. The slogan over the workers' heads reads, 'Produce more tanks for the Front!' The poster on the right says, 'Soldier of the Red Army, save us!'

As a result of such measures, Soviet factories poured out aircraft, tanks, guns and shells throughout the war. A leading Soviet general later wrote that:

SOURCE 21

The heroic feat of evacuation and rebuilding of industry during the war meant as much for the country's destiny as the greatest battles of the war.

G. K. Zhukov, *The Memoirs of Marshal Zhukov*, 1971

The British economy

The war also gave work to millions of unemployed British people. In Britain, however, there was more work than workers. In other words, there was a shortage of labour, especially of skilled labour in industries such as engineering.

The British government took many measures to overcome the labour shortage. One was to employ women in jobs normally given to men at that time. This was done after 1941 by conscripting women. It was the first time in any country that this had been done. Unmarried women between 19 and 30 had either to join a service such as the Wrens or Civil Defence, or do essential war work in industry. Source 22 shows women in one of the most essential industries of all: munitions.

Despite such measures, the labour shortage continued throughout the war. Output in some industries steadily fell. By the end of the war the British economy was exhausted.

SOURCE 22

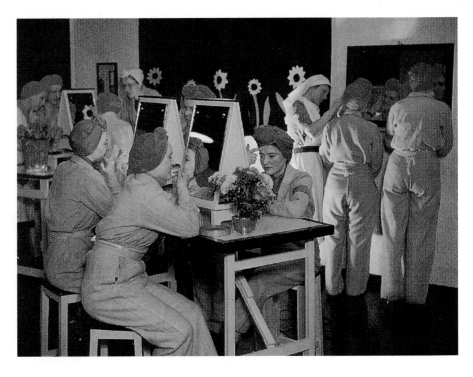

British munitions workers in a Royal Ordnance factory in November 1943. They were not putting on make-up but a special cream to stop their skin from absorbing explosive powders which can turn the skin yellow. They wore fire-resistant tunics, fire-proof turbans and rubber-soled shoes as safety precautions.

Under the bombs

> **i** **Bombs** *There were many different sizes, shapes and types of bomb, but only two basic kinds:* incendiary bombs *filled with petrol-based chemicals designed to set buildings on fire, and* high explosive bombs *designed to blow things up. Gas bombs, for protection against which people carried gas masks for much of the war, were never used.*

activity

1 Look closely at source 23.
a Make a list of things that were destroyed or damaged by bombs.
b For each kind of damage you have listed, say how the British hoped it would help them win the war.

In three countries at war – Britain, Germany and Japan – factory workers and other civilians in big towns and cities were bombed regularly from the air. Civilians were also sometimes bombed in parts of China, France, Italy and Romania.

Why were civilians bombed?

When the war began, each side tried using 'precision bombing' to hit targets such as ports, factories or railway junctions. The aim was to destroy the enemy's trade and industry, making it impossible for them to fight. This did not work. Bombs often did not hit their targets and, when they did, the damage was not always severe. As the war went on, both sides therefore started bombing whole towns and cities rather than just military or industrial targets. The British called this 'area bombing'.

Area bombing caused massive destruction. American and British planes dropped 2,697,473 tonnes of bombs on 131 German cities. Half fell on housing areas, killing 800,000 civilians, destroying 3.6 million homes and making 7.5 million people homeless. Source 23 shows the effects of area bombing on one of those cities.

SOURCE 23

Cologne (Köln) at the end of the war in 1945. Closer to Britain than most German cities, it was bombed heavily from 1941 onwards. In the heaviest raid, on 30 May 1942, over a thousand British bombers killed 486 people and destroyed 59,000 homes. By 1945 the population had dropped from a pre-war 700,000 to 25,000.

Area bombing hit the Japanese even harder than the Germans. Japanese houses were built close together and most were made of wood. This meant that fires started by bombs quickly spread across whole districts. On 10 March 1945, American planes dropped 1,700 tonnes of bombs on the small houses and shops of Tokyo's riverside districts. In a single night, 83,793 people died as fires raced through the streets. More than a quarter of a million buildings were burned down. In the week that followed four other cities were bombed just as heavily. The Japanese called it 'slaughter bombing'.

What was it like to be bombed?

A bombing raid was a terrifying experience for anyone in the target area, as source 24 shows. It is a description by Len Jones, a Londoner then aged 18, of the first minutes of a German air raid on London in September 1940.

SOURCE 24

The suction and the compression from the high explosive blasts just pulled you and pushed you, and the whole of the atmosphere was turbulating so hard that, after the explosion of a nearby bomb, you could actually feel your eyeballs being sucked out. I was holding my eyes to try and stop them going. And the suction was so vast, it ripped my shirt away, and ripped my trousers. Then I couldn't get my breath, the smoke was like acid and everything round me was black and yellow.

Joanna Mack and Steve Humphries, *London at War*, 1985

Len Jones was lucky. He found his way to an air-raid shelter and survived. But in every air-raid there were many who did not escape. People could be crushed when buildings collapsed, cut to pieces by sharp fragments flying through the air, or burned to death in fires. Some bombing raids were so heavy that they created **firestorms**. The first firestorm of the war took place in the German city of Hamburg when British bombers carried out continuous raids for ten days in the summer of 1943. Sources 25 and 26 show some of its effects.

SOURCE 25

People jumped into the canals and waterways and remained swimming or standing up to their necks in water for hours until the heat should die down. Even these suffered burns on their heads. They had to wet their faces constantly or they perished in the heat. The firestorm swept over the water with its heat and its showers of sparks so that even thick wooden posts burned down to the level of the water ... Children were torn away from their parents' hands by the force of the hurricane and whirled into the fire.

From a report by Hamburg's Chief of Police, written in December 1943

> **i** **Firestorms** *Heat rises, so the air above a burning building rises. The rising air is replaced by cooler air rushing in from outside. This fans the flames and makes the fire hotter, so the air above rises faster and faster. The cooler air that replaces it becomes a hurricane-force wind which can uproot trees and overturn cars. Winds as strong as that superheat the flames so that everything which can be burnt is totally consumed by fire. The worst firestorms of the war took place in Hamburg (1943), Dresden (1945) and Tokyo (1945).*

SOURCE 26

A street in Hamburg after a British air raid on the night of 27/28 July 1943. These people suffocated to death when fires burning at temperatures of 1,000 degrees Celsius used up so much oxygen that they could not breathe.

SOURCE 27

These German families lost their homes and possessions in an air raid and were living out of doors when this photograph was taken. The clothes on the rail behind them were for swappping with other homeless families without belongings.

activity

1 The people in sources 27 and 28 lost their homes and all their belongings. Make a list of ways in which you think their lives had to change as a result of this.
2 Sir Arthur Harris wrote (source 29) that bombing was 'a comparatively humane method'.
a What does 'humane' mean?
b How far do the sources and information on pages 78–81 agree with his point of view? Explain your answer.

Life for the people who survived heavy bombing raids was often very different from their usual way of life. Klaus Schmidt, who lived in Darmstadt in Germany, described what his city was like after a British air raid in 1944.

SOURCE 28

The hospitals were crammed. All preparations counted for nothing. You could travel without a ticket on the train, bicycle on the pavements. There were no windows in the trains, no schools, no doctors, no post, no telephone. One felt completely cut off from the world. To meet a friend who survived was a wonderful experience. There was no water, no light, no fire. A candle was of priceless value. Little children collected wood from the ruins for cooking. Every family dug its own latrine [toilet] in the garden.

Klaus Schmidt, *Die Brandnacht (Night of Fire)*, 1965

The man who organised the bombing of Germany, Sir Arthur Harris, later wrote that he did not regret it:

SOURCE 29

In spite of all that happened at Hamburg, bombing proved a comparatively humane method. For one thing, it saved the youth of this country and of our allies from being mown down by the military in the field, as it was in Flanders in the war of 1914–18. But the point is often made that bombing is especially wicked because it causes casualties among civilians. This is true, but then all wars have caused casualties among civilians.

Sir Arthur Harris, *Bomber Offensive*, 1947

assignments

1 Use the information in Part 6 to make a list of ways in which civilians' lives changed under wartime conditions between 1939 and 1945.

2 Give examples of the kinds of people whose lives
a changed greatly during the war, and
b changed only slightly during the war.

3 Some of the changes you have read about were changes in people's personal lives. Some changes affected whole communities. Some affected entire countries. Give examples of each under the headings 'personal changes', 'local changes' and 'national changes'.

4 Many of the changes you have listed led to suffering and unhappiness, and made people's lives worse than in peacetime. Were any of the changes improvements? Explain your answer.

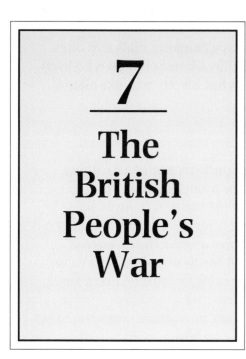

7
The British People's War

When they looked back in later years, many people remembered the Second World War as an important time in Britain's history. Even today, many survivors remember it as a time when they worked together in a common cause. They remember people facing danger with courage and good humour. They remember how they put up with hard work and discomfort and eventually won the war. Some remember the war as a *good* time in our country's history.

Are such memories accurate? Or are some of them myths – stories which many people believe but which are only partly true? The sources in Part 7 have been chosen to help you decide for yourself.

Evacuation

SOURCE 1

A group of evacuee children wait for their train to leave King's Cross station in London on 1 September. Find their identity labels and gas mask boxes, and look at their feet.

1 Look at source 1 and make brief notes about:

● how the children were dressed
● the things they were carrying with them,
● the expressions on their faces,
● the way they seemed to be behaving.

2 What does this photograph make you think about evacuation in 1939?

activity

3 Use sources 2 and 4 to explain why some children found evacuation a difficult experience.

4 What does source 3 make you think life was like for evacuated children in the countryside?

Many people now in their fifties and sixties have strong memories of being evacuated.

Mass evacuation began on 1 September 1939. Around two million people made their own arrangements. They went, for example, to stay with friends or relations. Slightly under 1.5 million women and children were evacuated by the government. Many were from poor working-class families who could not afford to evacuate themselves. Press photographers took thousands of pictures of them being evacuated. Source 1 is typical of the scenes they photographed.

Many of the children had never been in a train before. As source 2 shows, some were bewildered by what they saw from the windows. It was written in the 1980s by Tommy McSorley, aged 7 when he was evacuated from Glasgow in 1939.

SOURCE 2

As the train started moving forward there was a mighty roar from every compartment ... After about half an hour though, the train went dead quiet, for on looking out of the window everything had suddenly turned to green ... I think for the remainder of the journey I sat with my eyes tightly closed in fear, and it seemed every time I opened them I was surrounded by mountains and very strange animals I had never seen before ... I felt they would at any time gang together to attack the train and devour the passengers. It was a good deal later I discovered they were sheep.

Quoted in Ben Wicks, *No Time To Wave Goodbye*, 1988

When children reached their destinations in the countryside, they were taken to reception centres such as the local school or village hall. There, local people chose which ones they wanted to have as foster-children, and took them home. Over the next few weeks the press printed photographs like source 3 showing children having a good time in the country.

SOURCE 3

Evacuated children gathering blackberries in Buckinghamshire in autumn, 1939.

activity

1 Judging by source 4, does source 3 give a realistic impression of life in the country for evacuated children? Explain your answer.

i The **National Federation of Women's Institutes** was the largest women's organisation in the United Kingdom. Local Women's Institutes consisted mostly of middle-class and upper-class women who organised educational, social and charity events.

But for children like Mary Baxter, then aged eleven, the countryside was far from fun.

SOURCE 4

I was placed in a workman's cottage and woke up on my first morning to the screams of a pig. I looked out of my window and saw several people beating the animal with sticks and there was a horny-handed yokel cutting the pig's throat at the same time. It was their method of killing pigs. When I asked about it later, after the shock of witnessing it, they told me that beating a pig got its circulation going so the meat would be whiter.

The foster mum thought she was on to a very good thing with me and the other eleven year old girl billeted with her. I think she regarded it as a business transaction. We were expected to shop and wash up and look after a whining three year old . . . I got my own back by teaching the three year old some fruity London street terms. This was one way of repaying the lady of the house for all the drudgery she was subjecting me to.

Mary Baxter, interviewed in 1988 by Ruth Inglis in *The Children's War*, 1989

It wasn't only the children who found evacuation a difficult experience. Foster parents also found it hard. Many complained about children from slum areas in the big cities. The **National Federation of Women's Institutes** collected complaints from 1,700 Institutes across the country, and published them in a report. Source 6 is typical of what they said.

SOURCE 5

In practically every batch of children there were some who suffered from head-lice, skin diseases and bed-wetting . . . Some children [from Manchester] had never slept in beds . . . One boy [from Salford] had never had a bath before; his ribs looked as black as if black-leaded . . . The state of the children [from Liverpool] was such that the school had to be fumigated after reception . . .

Bread and lard are a usual breakfast for a number of [Walthamstow] children when at home . . . Few Manchester children would eat food that demanded the use of teeth – could only eat with a teaspoon . . . One little girl of five [from Liverpool] remarked that she would like to have beer and cheese for supper . . . Some [Gosport] children had never used a knife and fork. The [Finsbury] children did not understand sitting down for a meal but seemed to like the food in the hand.

National Federation of Women's Institutes, *Town People Through Country Eyes*, 1941

The report was exaggerated. The Women's Institutes later admitted that only a small proportion of evacuated children were like that. But this did not stop rumours flying around. Many worried householders did all they could to avoid taking children into their homes. Doreen Holloway from Battersea in London remembered:

SOURCE 6

The house that we were evacuated to was enormous, at least by our standards. We rarely saw the lady of the house, and were put in the care of two servants who obviously resented us. You know, we felt the resentment from the beginning. We had to sleep on sacks filled with straw outside the kitchen, although at the time there were spare beds upstairs in the house ... My parents were never asked inside when they came to visit us, they had to wait outside the fence in the street.

Quoted in Joanna Mack and Steve Humphries, *London at War*, 1985

Officials who ran the evacuation scheme were soon having difficulty finding homes for poor children. *Picture Post*, a popular magazine of the time, printed a story about the evacuation problem in November 1940. It reported that evacuees were more likely to get a welcome from poor people than from wealthy people with big houses. It illustrated the story with the picture in source 7.

SOURCE 7

The original caption for this photograph said: "How the poor are helping ... Mr Brooks is a miner with a family of seven and a five roomed house. With him are billeted Mr and Mrs Lemmerman and their four children from London."

activity

2 How can sources 5, 6 and 7 be used to suggest that there were big differences between working-class and upper-class people in 1939?

3 The report quoted in source 5 was collected from 1,700 Women's Institutes in all parts of Britain. Does this mean it was an accurate picture of what poor children from British cities were like in 1939?

4 Source 7 and source 3 are both photographs of evacuees.

a How do they differ in the way they picture evacuees?

b Which do you think is the more useful as evidence of the conditions in which evacuees lived? Explain your answer.

5 Sources 2, 4 and 6 are from the memoirs of people who were children in 1939. They wrote or recorded their memoirs many years after the events they describe. Does this affect their value or reliability? Explain your answer.

The Dunkirk spirit

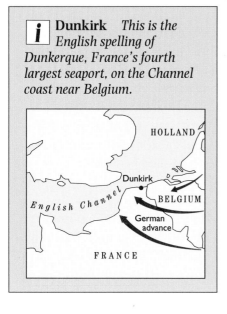

i **Dunkirk** *This is the English spelling of Dunkerque, France's fourth largest seaport, on the Channel coast near Belgium.*

Evacuation from Dunkirk

Many British people who lived through the Second World War shared something which they called 'the Dunkirk spirit'.

Dunkirk was in the headlines of every British newspaper during the first few days of June 1940. Only ten days before, German armed forces had invaded France and forced the French and British armies facing them to retreat to the English Channel. Nearly half a million British and French soldiers were now trapped there between the sea and the German army.

In an attempt to save the trapped soldiers, the British navy organised a sea-borne rescue operation. Several hundred destroyers, minesweepers and other warships were sent to the French coast in 'Operation Dynamo'. They were helped by volunteers in hundreds of small boats such as trawlers, tugs and river boats. Between 26 May and 4 June, 865 boats rescued 215,587 British soldiers and 127,031 French soldiers from Dunkirk.

This was an amazing achievement. The Prime Minister, Winston Churchill, had expected only thirty thousand to be saved. Ten times that number were rescued. However, as sources 8 and 9 show, the soldiers left behind them a huge amount of equipment and arrived home filthy and exhausted. Worse, 68,111 soldiers had been killed or taken prisoner.

SOURCE 8

British soldiers at Dover walk off a Royal Navy destroyer that rescued them from Dunkirk on 1 June 1940.

SOURCE 9

	Shipped to France	Used in action, destroyed or left behind	Brought back to England
Guns	2,794	2,472	322
Vehicles	68,618	63,879	4,739
Motor cycles	21,081	20,548	533
Ammunition (tons)	109,000	76,697	32,303
Supplies and stores (tons)	449,000	415,940	33,060
Petrol (tons)	166,000	164,929	1,071

Major L. F. Ellis, *The War in France and Flanders 1939–40*, 1953

The soldiers did not expect much of a welcome when they reached Britain. 'I wasn't looking forward to our arrival,' said one. 'I thought we'd be shot,' said another. The soldiers were therefore amazed by their reception. Cheering crowds lined the railway from Dover to London to watch them pass. News reports like source 10 described them as heroes.

SOURCE 10

News report from the *Bristol Evening Post*, 31 May 1940.

activity

1 Look at sources 8 and 9.
a What do they tell you about the British army in June 1940?
b Why do you think many soldiers did not expect a welcome when they returned to Britain?
2a Look at source 10, then make a list of words, phrases or sentences that give a favourable impression of the British army.
b Try to find any words, phrases or sentences that give an unfavourable impression.

SOURCE 11

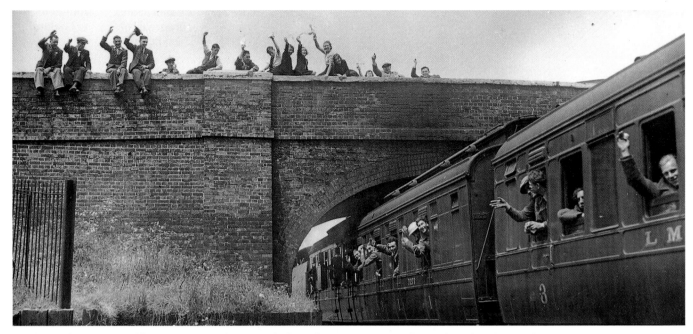

Local people wave to soldiers returning from Dunkirk as their train passes through Paddock Wood in Kent on 1 June 1940.

Hundreds of trains like the one in source 11 took the soldiers to rest centres all over Britain. Everywhere they were treated like heroes. Source 12, written by a Sergeant-Major who was sent to recover in Burton-in-Trent, is typical of their experiences.

SOURCE 12

A lady stopped me in the street and asked me if I had come from France; when I replied that I had, she gave me a shirt and a packet of Woodbines (cigarettes). At a nearby pub I asked if I could phone my wife; the landlord took charge, got the number for me and refused to accept any payment.

Things were organised for us in Burton-on-Trent as though we were heroes. We were taken on a bus tour, had an evening out at a working man's club, were entertained by the bowls club – and all for free.

Robert Jackson, *Dunkirk: The British Evacuation,* 1976

On 4 June, Winston Churchill told Parliament that the army had returned safely. But after praising the soldiers he said that Dunkirk was a 'colossal military disaster'. He warned that Britain was now almost defenceless if the Germans invaded. He finished by saying:

SOURCE 13

We shall defend our island, whatever the cost may be, we shall fight on the beaches, we shall fight on the landing grounds, we shall fight in the fields and in the streets, we shall fight in the hills; we shall never surrender.

Parliamentary Debates, 4 June 1940

activity

1 The soldiers who returned from Dunkirk did not expect to be welcomed. Why do you think they felt like that?
2 Sources 11 and 12 show that they did get a good welcome. How can this be explained?

Defending the island

activity

4 Look at sources 14 and 15. Make a list of the ways in which civilians prepared to defend Britain against an invasion.

5 How did the writer of source 14 feel about these defences?

Defending Britain against an invasion was easier said than done. Germany had two hundred army divisions just across the Channel. Britain had only 27 divisions to repel them. They had left so much equipment behind at Dunkirk, that some now had to borrow old guns from local museums and hire buses to travel around the country.

Civilians were therefore asked to help defend Britain. A quarter of a million civilians had already joined a force known as the Local Defence Volunteers (LDV). They hurriedly set to work building whatever defences they could. Sources 14 and 15 give us an idea of the effect this had on the country.

SOURCE 14

Tuesday 16 July 1940

The fear of invasion hangs over every minute of the day . . . It is the preparations for meeting an army among the fields around us, at home, that fill us with dread. The meadows beyond the Iron Bridge over the railway . . . are scarred with long trenches and mounds to prevent the landing of any planes or gliders . . . Concrete gun-emplacements ('pill-boxes') have been created . . . Old Fords full of bricks are left by the wayside ready to be shoved broadside on into the roads . . . The names on post offices, signposts, on railway stations and AA call boxes have been obliterated. Steel helmets are carried by every other man.

George Beardmore, *Civilians at War. Journals 1938-46*, 1984

SOURCE 15

This photograph, taken on 5 June 1940, shows how people in a village in Northumberland made a roadblock with old carts, fences, railings and other odds and ends from nearby farms.

The Local Defence Volunteers were also expected to fight the Germans if they invaded. Some people, however, questioned whether they would be able to put up much of a fight. Many were over forty, the age limit for army service, and few had weapons or even uniforms. This description of the LDV in a Sussex village is typical of LDV units all over Britain in May and June 1940.

SOURCE 16

There were shepherds, farm hands, gardeners, village shopkeepers, a retired civil servant from India, a retired schoolmaster, and one or two folk who worked in London . . . Men came in from their work in the fields, and we stood round a waggon in a farmyard and discussed things . . . Then came the 'election of officers', which was a serious and difficult matter. The local section leader must obviously be a chap always there in the village, so the choice fell on Roy, mine host at the pub. 'He's the best rabbit shot in the neighbourhood,' said one of his backers.

Charles Graves, *The Home Guard of Britain*, 1943

In July, the government renamed the LDV the Home Guard. But behind their backs, many people called the Home Guard 'Dad's Army' and made fun of it. Incidents like those shown in source 17 and described in source 18 help us understand why.

SOURCE 17

A Home Guard unit arrest two men pretending to be German agents in a training exercise in 1940.

SOURCE 18

I was woken up in the early hours of the morning by the tolling of the church bell, and a shrill voice shouting below my bedroom window 'Invasion, sir, invasion!' . . . In rushed a Home Guard in a state of great excitement. 'They are landing on the beach, sir, there's hundreds of them.' I told him to wait a moment while I collected one or two stalwarts [supporters] . . . When I returned I found the messenger had gone, and so we were forced to grope our way through the sandhills without the help of a guide. We had not gone very far before we heard some terrible cursing and swearing just in front of us and there was the missing runner with his foot caught in a rabbit snare . . . After we had set him free we set off again, and a moment or two later we were peeping over the top of a sandhill not far from the beach. I crept alongside the lookout man who whispered 'There they are, sir, hundreds of them.' There were hundreds of them, but they were not Germans. 'You silly ass,' I said, 'don't you know what those are? They are stakes placed on the beach to stop German aeroplanes landing at low tide.'

The commander of a Home Guard unit quoted in Norman Longmate, *The Home Front.
An Anthology of Personal Experience 1938-1945*, 1981

As you have read, the Germans did not invade Britain and so the Home Guard never had to fight the German army. But does this mean it was useless? Source 19 shows how one historian has answered that question.

SOURCE 19

Their value to the defence of Great Britain was unquestionable. Apart from weapons and equipment, the army's greatest need throughout the summer was for weapons and training; and training was impossible while . . . there were 5,000 miles of coast to watch . . . road blocks to man, and bridges to protect . . . For all these duties the Home Guard was available. Had it not been, an almost intolerable strain would have been placed on the Home Forces.

Peter Fleming, *Invasion 1940*, 1958

activity

1 You are one of Winston Churchill's advisers in July 1940. Use sources 14, 15, 16, 17 and 18 to prepare brief notes advising him about how well prepared the Home Guard was to defend Britain against a German invasion.
2a How does source 17 suggest that the Home Guard was better equipped to fight Germans than when it was first set up?
b Does source 18 support the view suggested by source 17?
3 Judging by sources 16–19, did the Home Guard deserve to be made fun of and called Dad's Army?

The Battle of Britain

Hitler did not think that the British were in a mood to fight in June 1940, so he offered to make peace on lenient terms. Churchill rejected the offer and said that Britain would fight on. Hitler therefore ordered his armed forces to invade Britain.

The first stage of the invasion was carried out by the German Air Force. Its orders were to destroy the Royal Air Force so that British planes could not attack ships bringing German soldiers across the Channel. Throughout the summer of 1940 German and British pilots fought each other in aircraft battles high above southern England (sources 20 and 21). The fighting was fiercest in the last two weeks of August when the Germans attacked the RAF's airfields. By the start of September the RAF was close to defeat. Its airfields were badly damaged and it did not have enough pilots.

On 7 September, however, the Germans stopped attacking the airfields and started bombing London instead. This was in revenge for British air raids on Berlin. It gave the RAF a chance to recover its strength and reorganise its forces.

SOURCE 20

The Battle of Britain, painted in 1941 by Paul Nash, a leading war artist, shows British and German aircraft fighting over the River Thames in August 1940. The English Channel and France are in the background.

SOURCE 21

Fight over Portland, painted in summer 1940 by Richard Eurich, another leading **war artist**. The artist went to Portland, a naval base on the English Channel, every day during the Battle of Britain to paint this scene.

i **War artists** *were appointed by a government body, the War Artists' Advisory Committee, to record important events and activities in the war at home and abroad.*

A week later, flying in different, larger formations, the RAF shot down sixty German aircraft on a bombing raid over London. From then on, the Germans stopped daytime bombing raids and went over to night bombing.

This meant that the RAF had kept control of the air space over Britain, and could still attack any invading force. Hitler was forced to cancel his invasion plans. The RAF had won the 'Battle of Britain'.

activity

1a War artists had the job of recording important scenes or events in the war. Why do you think both Paul Nash and Richard Eurich decided to paint the scenes in sources 20 and 21?

b Paul Nash's painting (source 20) is about real events but it isn't painted realistically.
 (i) Give examples of lack of realism in the painting.
 (ii) How does source 21 seem more realistic?
 (iii) Does Paul Nash's lack of realism mean that source 20 is less valuable than source 21 as evidence of the Battle of Britain?

2 What do these paintings make you think or feel about the Battle of Britain? Explain your answer.

The Blitz

When the Germans bombed London on 7 September, it was only the first of many air raids. For the next nine months, people in every major British city were bombed in a series of devastating night attacks. They called it the Blitz.

The Blitz had three aims: to disrupt transport by bombing railways; to damage industry and trade by bombing factories and ports; and to destroy people's **morale** by bombing their homes.

Although the Blitz did a great deal of damage, many of the people who survived said that it did not destroy their morale. Some said that it did the opposite, that it brought people together in a spirit of shared danger and hardship. How true was this?

Air raid precautions

From the first day of the war, local authorities had made plans to protect the cities from air raids. Strict 'black-out' rules banned the use of car headlights, street lamps or any other light that bombers might see from the air. Air-raid sirens gave warnings of aircraft approaching. An organisation called ARP (Air Raid Precautions) was set up, with wardens, firemen, nurses and rescue workers. Air-raid shelters were built in streets, gardens and parks. By the time the Blitz started, people like those in source 22 had grown used to taking shelter when German aircraft were overhead.

SOURCE 22

Families in an air-raid shelter in August 1940, just before the start of the Blitz.

London in the Blitz

Nothing, however, had prepared people for the sheer scale of the Blitz. In the first raid on London on 7 September 1940, 250 aircraft rained 330 tonnes of bombs on the East End of the city. This was the poorest and most overcrowded part of London. The bombs killed 430 people, injured 1,600 and destroyed thousands of homes. When the bombers returned the next day they killed 400 more. So it went on for 76 days in succession.

The attacks terrified many East Enders. Some panicked. On 10 September officials wrote in a top-secret report to the government:

SOURCE 23

Increased tension everywhere and when the siren goes people run madly for shelters with white faces ... Citizens Advice Bureau is inundated with mothers and young children hysterical and asking to be removed from the district ... Exodus from East End growing rapidly. Taxi drivers report taking party after party to Euston and Paddington [stations] with belongings.

Home Intelligence Report by the Ministry of Information, 10 September 1940

SOURCE 24

Families of Londoners shelter from bombs in the Elephant and Castle tube station on the night of 11 November 1940.

As the air raids continued, many families looked for shelter in the London Underground, or 'tube' (source 24). Emily Eary, then 23 years old, remembered in an interview (source 25) what it was like to shelter there in the early days of the Blitz.

SOURCE 25

People would rush to get to the tubes, almost knock you over to get down the escalator, because ... people were getting panic-stricken to get down there, to get out of the noise, to get out of the devastation ... We lived like rats underground ... You'd queue for hours to get a good spot on the platform – you'd want to avoid the cold, draughty, smelly parts. People spread newspapers on the floor or left bundles on the floor to show where it was their territory, and somebody might come and kick them away and that would lead to arguments over who should be there. Sometimes you'd get people squaring up, and fights.

Jane Waller and Michael Vaughan-Rees, *Blitz. The Civilian War 1940-1945*, 1990

The government was worried that panic might spread, so it stopped the press from reporting bad news about the air raids. Films or photographs showing dead bodies were banned. Press reports which gave the number of dead and injured were censored. Any film of a bombed street had to finish with a building that was still standing. The rest of the country therefore did not get to hear about the worst horrors of the bombing. The stories they read and pictures like source 29 showed instead how well London was 'taking it'.

SOURCE 26

A family of East Enders rescue their belongings from their bomb-damaged house.

activity

I Look at sources 24 and 26. What do they make you think or feel about London people during the Blitz?
2 Do sources 23 and 25 change the way the photographs make you feel? Explain your answer.
3 Which pair of sources do you consider is most useful as evidence of how people behaved in the Blitz? Explain your answer.

The Blitz on Britain

In November 1940 German bombers started massed raids on cities in the rest of Britain. In the heaviest raid, 437 bombers attacked Coventry on the night of 14–15 November, killing 380 people and destroying the city centre (Source 28). Heavy raids followed on Birmingham, Bristol, Merseyside, Southampton, Sheffield, Manchester, Portsmouth, Cardiff, Swansea, Clydeside, Hull, Plymouth and Belfast.

One of the hardest-hit cities was Liverpool. Eight days of bombing caused so much damage that the army and police cordoned off the city while the wreckage was cleared. Nobody was allowed to enter unless they had essential business. People jumped to the conclusion that dreadful things were happening there. Rumours spread like wildfire. A man in the town of Leek, fifty miles away, wrote down the rumours he heard there.

SOURCE 27

General morale: *Very unsteady. This has been a week of gruesome rumours which were briefly as follows – Train loads of unidentified corpses have been sent from Merseyside for mass cremation.*
(2) Martial law has had to be put into operation in several heavily-raided industrial areas. (3) Homeless and hungry people have marched around in bombed areas, carrying white flags and howling protests. (4) Food riots are taking place.

Mass Observation no. 706, Report on Liverpool, 22 May 1941

SOURCE 28

People sort out their belongings in a street in Coventry after the air raid of 14–15 November 1940.

The Blitz ended in the summer of 1941. German bombers were needed for the invasion of Russia (see page 42) so all but four of the forty-four aircraft squadrons were sent to the other side of Europe.

This was not an end to all bombing. Even with their reduced force of planes, the Germans continued to make air raids. In 1942, for example, they bombed Britain's most beautiful cities in a series of 'Baedeker raids'. Named after the Baedeker tourist guidebooks, these attacks were in retaliation for British massed air raids on Germany. Large areas of Exeter, Bath, Norwich, York and Canterbury were flattened.

Finally, in 1944, south-east England was hit by a new kind of Blitz when Germany bombed it with V-1 aircraft. The V-1 was a small, pilotless jet plane carrying a tonne of high explosive, fired from launching ramps across the Channel. In September 1944 Londoners were also hit by V-2 rockets, each carrying four tonnes of high explosive. By the time the war ended in May 1945, nearly six thousand V-1s and one thousand V-2s had fallen in the south-east. Nearly 9,000 civilians were killed and 35,000 were injured in these attacks.

assignments

Sources 29–31 are about Britain during the Second World War. Source 29 comes from a book about the war written by a famous wartime entertainer, Vera Lynn, for the fiftieth anniversary of the start of the war.

SOURCE 29

The spirit of Britons during World War Two was of . . . optimism, quiet courage, enterprise, patience and uncrushable humour.

Vera Lynn with Robin Cross, *We'll Meet Again*, 1989

Source 30 is from an interview in 1984 with Professor Arthur Ling. During the war he was an architect working for the City of London.

SOURCE 30

People were much more together. They met in the air-raid shelters, in the tubes at night, they were in the Home Guard, or they queued for Spam or whatever it was they could get hold of, one egg a week. Everybody really lost a lot of their inhibitions about talking to their next door neighbours. When the raids were over they used to almost celebrate in the early morning and this was the spirit that I think a lot of people hoped would continue after the war.

Quoted in Paul Addison, *Now the War is Over*, 1985

Source 31 was written by a leading British historian who specialises in twentieth-century British social history.

SOURCE 31

Much of what has been written about the Home Front in the Second World War is myth rather than history. This is perfectly understandable. The war was a very powerful experience for all who lived through it. At the time . . . the mass media were mobilised in the direction of presenting certain aspects of the war and suppressing others. Looking back, people tend to remember what they want to remember, and to suppress the less pleasant parts of the war experience.

Arthur Marwick, *The Home Front*, 1976

1a Sources 29 and 30 say similar things about Britain in the Second World War. Briefly summarise in your own words what they say.
b How is source 31 different in what it says about the war?

2 Sources 29–31 are a mixture of facts and opinions.
a Which source contains only opinions?
b Give examples from one of the other sources of statements that you think are facts.

3 Look at sources 24, 27, 29 and 31. Many photographs like sources 24, 27 and 29 were published in newspapers and magazines during the war. Photographs like source 31 were not, because they were censored. How might this have affected the way in which people like Vera Lynn (source 29) and Arthur Ling (source 30) later wrote about how British people behaved during the war?

4 Look at sources 26, 28 and 31. How do these sources differ from sources 29 and 30 in what they say about British people during the war?

5 In source 31 Arthur Marwick says that much of what has been written about Britain in the Second World War is 'myth rather than history'.
a What is a myth?
b How does a myth differ from a historical event?
c Judging by what you have read in Part 7, how was it possible for myths about the war to spread?

6a Choose at least one source from Part 7 that agrees with the opinions of the authors in sources 29 and 30.
b Choose at least one source which disagrees with them.

7 Judging by all you have found out about Britain at war, which interpretation do you find most convincing? Explain your answer.

Fifty million people were killed in the Second World War, most of them civilians. To put it another way, someone died violently every three and a half seconds, every day and night for six years between 1939 and 1945. Millions more suffered injury and hardship of every kind. What made this war so destructive and painful?

The Holocaust

Nearly six million of the people who died were European Jews. They were killed by Nazis in a series of events known as the **Holocaust**.

The Jews of Europe

Jews had lived in Europe for over a thousand years. Originally they lived in the Middle East but were expelled from their homeland by the Romans. Forced to move to other countries, they settled all over Europe as well as in Russia and north Africa.

Wherever they settled, Jews were likely to be treated badly. In some countries they were not allowed to own land. In others they had to live in a separate part of town called a ghetto or wear special clothes. From time to time mobs attacked and killed them.

This ill-treatment of Jews is called **anti-semitism** and it was one of the main features of Nazi Germany. Nazis believed that people were divided into races and that some races were 'superior' to others. In Nazi eyes, the Germans were a 'master race' of Aryans (source 1). They wanted to keep the Aryan race 'pure' by staying apart from other races, especially Jews, whom they called an 'inferior' race.

> **i** The word **Holocaust** comes from the Greek words holos and kaustos which literally mean 'completely burnt'. In general, the word can be used to describe any large-scale killing and destruction, especially by fire. But it is most often used to describe the persecution and mass murder of Jews by German Nazis between 1933 and 1945.

> **i** A **Semite** is someone who belongs to any of the peoples of south–west Asia, especially Jews and Arabs. In Nazi Germany the word was used to describe Jewish people only. **Anti-semitism** therefore came to mean hatred of and bad treatment of Jewish people.

Nazi laws against German Jews

The Nazis started treating Jews badly as soon as they took power in 1933. They stopped people from using Jewish shops. They sacked Jews from government jobs. And from 1935 onwards they introduced laws which restricted the lives of Jews by taking away their rights. Source 2 shows some of those laws.

SOURCE 1

A poster showing the kinds of men Nazis thought belonged to the Aryan race: 'Nordic', 'Falian', 'Eastern Baltic', 'Western', 'Dinaric' and 'Eastern'.

SOURCE 2

The Reich law on citizenship, 15 September 1935
A citizen of the Reich is a subject who has only German blood...
The law for the protection of German blood and honour, 15 September 1935
   I *Marriages between Jews and citizens of German ... blood are forbidden...*
  II *Sexual relations outside marriage between Jews and nationals of German or kindred blood are forbidden...*
Decree regarding the change of family names, 17 August 1938
Jews are allowed certain first names only ... Jews with first names different from those listed must use the first name 'Israel' (for men) and 'Sara' (for women) in addition to their own names.
Order by the Reich Minister of Education, 16 November 1938
Jews may only attend Jewish schools. All Jewish students not yet dismissed from German schools must be dismissed immediately.
Decree by the Berlin police, 3 December 1938
Jews are banned from all cinemas, shows, concert and lecture halls, museums, amusement places, sports fields, ...
Decree regarding identification badges for Jews, 1 September 1941
Jews over six years of age must wear the 'Star of David' when appearing in public. The 'Star of David' is a black, six-pointed star on yellow material ... with the inscription 'Jew'.

Reichsgesetzblatt (*The National Law Gazette*), 1935–1941

activity

1a You are a citizen of your country. What does this mean?
b What would you lose if your citizenship was taken away from you?
2 Study source 2.
a Describe how a Jewish person's life in Germany was changed by the laws and decrees in source 2.
b Which of these laws might have made it easier for some people in Germany to treat Jews badly? Explain your answer.

Organised violence against Jews

Jews in many parts of Germany tried to resist the Nazis but this resulted in worse treatment than before. In November 1938 a Jew shot dead a Nazi official. In retaliation, armed Nazis organised a campaign of terror against the Jewish population. They called it 'The Night of Broken Glass'. Ten thousand Jewish shopkeepers had their shop windows smashed and the contents stolen, and 191 synagogues were burned down. Ninety-one Jews were murdered and 20,000 were thrown into concentration camps.

Ghettoes

After the war began in 1939, Jews in countries conquered by the Germans also began to suffer in Nazi hands. From 1940 onwards, Jews in Poland were made to live in ghettoes – walled-off areas of towns or cities which they were not allowed to leave. The 400,000 Jews of Warsaw, a city of 1,200,000 people, were made to live in an area only a fiftieth the size of the city. Walled into this tiny area, and with no means of escape, tens of thousands of Warsaw Jews starved to death over the next four years. Many others were killed by cold or hunger.

SOURCE 3

In April 1943 the Jews of the Warsaw ghetto revolted against the German authorities. The Germans crushed the revolt by setting the ghetto on fire and expelling the inhabitants. 30,000 Jews like the families in this photograph taken on 25 April 1943 were sent to the extermination camp at Treblinka.

Mass murder in the Soviet Union

Nearly three million Jews lived in the western parts of the Soviet Union. When the German armies invaded the USSR in 1941, 'Special Action Groups' of soldiers followed them into the areas they occupied. Their orders were to kill the Jews in every occupied town and village.

The 'Special Action Groups' carried out their orders with dreadful efficiency. Whole communities of Jews were rounded up, made to take their clothes off, and then shot into mass graves.

The biggest of these mass murders was committed outside the city of Kiev. A Special Action Group rounded up 30,000 Jews living in Kiev and marched them to the edge of a ravine in a place called Babi Yar. Using machine guns, they shot their 30,000 prisoners into the ravine and then buried them by undermining the wall of the ravine to make a landslide.

Extermination

In 1942, when most of Europe and the western USSR was under German rule, the Nazi leaders decided to carry out what they called

SOURCE 4

A soldier from a Special Action Group in the act of murdering a Jewish mother and her child in the USSR in 1941.

SOURCE 5

These Jewish families had just arrived at Auschwitz when this photograph was taken. Shortly afterwards they were taken into the building shown in source 6 and murdered with poison gas.

'the final solution to the Jewish problem'. By this they meant the killing of every Jew in Europe, either by murder or by working them to death.

To kill an estimated 11 million Jews, the Nazis set up 'extermination camps' in remote areas of Poland. Each camp was linked to the rest of Europe by rail. Jews were transported to the camps in long trains of goods wagons that ferried backwards and forwards across Europe.

As soon as a train arrived at a camp, the passengers were divided into two groups: those who were to work and those who were to die. Sources 5, 6 and 7 give some idea of how this was done at the biggest camp – Auschwitz. The women and children were separated from the men. Guards then told them they must have showers for reasons of hygiene. After taking their clothes off they were herded into what they were told was a bath house. In fact, it was a gas chamber. Once the prisoners were inside, the guards locked the doors and poured crystals of a poisonous gas through a hole in the ceiling.

SOURCE 6

A watercolour, painted after 1945 by a former prisoner, W. Siwek, shows women at Auschwitz being selected for death in a gas chamber.

SOURCE 7

'Crematorium number 5' at Auschwitz extermination camp. After being killed in 'gas chambers' on the left, prisoners' bodies were burnt in ovens in the building on the right of the photograph.

Why did the prisoners not try to escape? Primo Levi, an Italian Jew who was selected to work at Auschwitz, and survived, explained:

SOURCE 8

In most cases the new arrivals did not know what awaited them. They were received with cold efficiency but without brutality, invited to undress 'for the showers'. Sometimes they were handed soap and towels and promised hot coffee after their showers. The gas chambers were, in fact, camouflaged as shower rooms, with pipes, faucets, dressing rooms, clothes hooks, benches, and so forth. When, instead, prisoners showed the smallest signs of suspecting their fate, the SS and their collaborators used . . . extreme brutality, with shouts, threats, kicks, shots, loosing their dogs, which were trained to tear prisoners to pieces, against people who were often confused, desperate, weakened by five or ten days of travelling in sealed railroad cars.

Primo Levi, afterword to *If This is a Man*, 1987

We do not know the exact number of Jews who were killed during the Second World War. The deaths shown on the map above were calculated by a historian called Martin Gilbert using five different kinds of evidence. He used records kept in government archives in Jerusalem, London and Washington. He used letters and

activity

1 Look at source 9.
a According to source 9, how many Jews were killed in the Holocaust?
b Which five countries suffered the greatest loss of Jews in the Holocaust?
2 Using the sources and information on pages 99–104, explain
a why and b how the Nazis killed so many Jews.

tape-recordings sent to him by survivors. He used a huge set of documents called the Nuremburg Documents, which were used as evidence in trials of Nazi leaders after the war. He used 'memorial books' about each murdered community prepared by survivors. And he used hundreds of secondary sources, such as books written by other historians. All these sources are public and so can be seen by anyone who wants to check the figures.

SOURCE 9

The Holocaust, 1939–1945

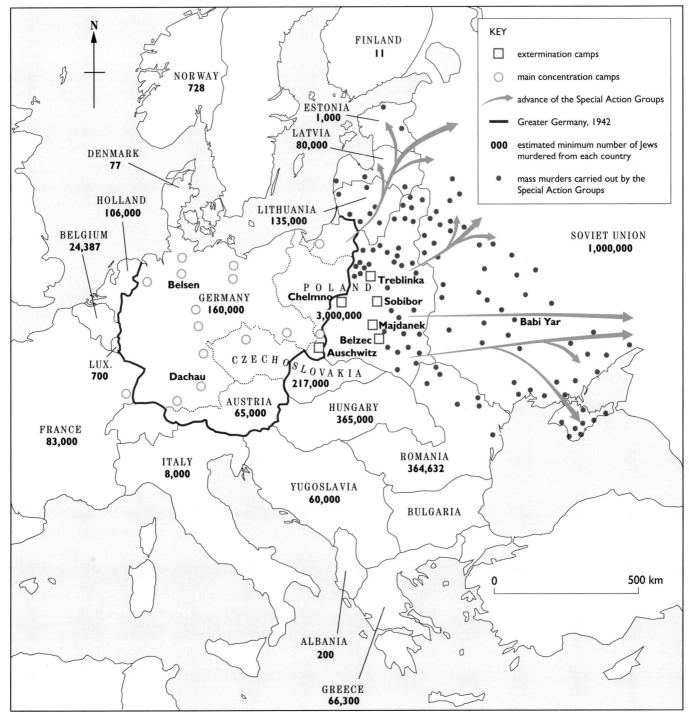

KEY

☐ extermination camps

◯ main concentration camps

➔ advance of the Special Action Groups

━━ Greater Germany, 1942

000 estimated minimum number of Jews murdered from each country

● mass murders carried out by the Special Action Groups

FINLAND **11**

NORWAY **728**

ESTONIA **1,000**

LATVIA **80,000**

DENMARK **77**

HOLLAND **106,000**

BELGIUM **24,387**

LITHUANIA **135,000**

Belsen

GERMANY **160,000**

POLAND **3,000,000**

Chelmno

Treblinka

Sobibor

Majdanek

Belzec

Auschwitz

Babi Yar

SOVIET UNION **1,000,000**

LUX. **700**

Dachau

CZECHOSLOVAKIA **217,000**

AUSTRIA **65,000**

HUNGARY **365,000**

FRANCE **83,000**

ITALY **8,000**

YUGOSLAVIA **60,000**

ROMANIA **364,632**

BULGARIA

ALBANIA **200**

GREECE **66,300**

0   500 km

Killing 'undesirables'

In addition to murdering six million Jews during the war, the Nazis also killed several million non-Jews who they said were 'undesirable'.

They began killing 'undesirables' in 1939 when Hitler ordered the use of euthanasia, or 'mercy killing', for incurably ill patients in hospital. Over the next two years more than 70,000 patients were killed by their doctors. After the invasion of Poland, 'mercy killings' were also carried out by SS troops who shot thousands of patients in Polish mental hospitals.

The Nazis also killed 'undesirables' whom they had been keeping in concentration camps. These included members of political parties which opposed them, homosexual men and members of certain religious groups such as Jehovah's Witnesses. Thousands of such prisoners were sent to the extermination camps in Poland.

Many 'undesirables' belonged to racial groups whom the Nazis disliked. They too were rounded up and sent to the gas chambers: a quarter of a million Gypsies and hundreds of thousands of Slavs from Russia and eastern Europe.

Organised massacres

Many civilians were killed in massacres carried out by soldiers. The first massacre of the war took place when the Japanese army invaded China at the end of 1937. After capturing the city of Nanjing, then the capital of China, Japanese soldiers killed 200,000 men, women and children in a slaughter lasting six weeks. Sasaki Toichi, commander of one of the Japanese brigades, later explained in his autobiography how it was possible for such a thing to happen:

SOURCE 10

Prisoners surrendered in droves, several thousand in all. Our enraged troops ignored superior orders and slaughtered one bunch after another. We had suffered heavy casualties in the bitter ten-day fighting. Many of our men had lost good friends. The unit hated the Chinese and there was a feeling of wanting to kill every one of the bastards.

Quoted in Saburo Ienaga, *Japan's Last War*, 1979

Massacres were often carried out by soldiers wanting revenge. In June 1942, German forces went to a village in Czechoslovakia called Lidice after resistance fighters had killed a leading Nazi official. They shot every man over the age of 16, sent all the women and children to concentration camps, and then destroyed the entire village. Exactly two years later, on 10 June 1944, German troops in France took revenge on a village called Oradour after resistance fighters shot one of their officers. Out of a population of 653 they shot 190 men dead, and burned to death 452 women and children by locking them in the parish church and setting it on fire.

Some massacres were carried out in cold blood. In 1939, for example, 4,500 Polish officers surrendered to the Soviet Army after the Polish army had been defeated. Instead of keeping them as prisoners of war, the Soviet secret police took them to a forest near a village called Katyn. With their hands tied behind their backs the officers were shot in the neck and thrown into mass graves.

Sieges and starvation

In wars throughout history, armies have laid siege to their enemies' cities, trying to starve them into surrender. The Second World War was no exception. Major sieges took place at Warsaw in Poland, Chongqing in China and Leningrad in the USSR. Towards the end of the war, entire countries were under siege, especially Japan which was almost entirely cut off by the Allies in 1945.

Starvation affected the way people behaved towards each other. Source 11, an extract from the diary of a Jewish girl in a ghetto in Poland, describes how hunger changed her behaviour.

SOURCE 11

Lodz, March 11, 1942: *There is nothing to eat, we are going to die of hunger. My teeth ache and I am very hungry, my left leg is frostbitten ... My mother looks terrible, a shadow of her former self ...*

I have no heart or pity, I eat everything I can lay my hands on. Today I had an argument with my father, I insulted and even cursed him. And this was because yesterday I weighed 20 decagrams of noodles but this morning took a spoonful for myself. When father came back at night, he weighed the noodles again. Of course there was less. He started yelling at me ... I was upset and I cursed him. Father just stood at the window and cried like a child. No stranger ever abused him like I did.

A. Adelson and R. Lapides (Eds), *Lodz Ghetto: Inside a Community under Siege*, 1989

The cruellest siege of the war was the Siege of Leningrad (now St Petersburg). For 900 days from 1941 to 1943 German troops surrounded the city and cut off nearly all its supplies. The city authorities rationed any food that got through so that everybody had a share, but the shares got smaller as time went on. By the winter of 1941–42 the ration for soldiers was 500 grams of bread a day, 250 for workers and 125 for everyone else. Source 12 shows how this affected one family.

A million people – that is, four out of every ten people – in Leningrad died of starvation during the siege. And this was only one city in the Soviet Union. Recent official figures now show that some 26 million Soviet people died as a direct result of the war, many of them the victims of starvation.

SOURCE 12

These pages are from the diary of the 11-year-old girl in the photograph, Tanya Savicheva. They say (from top left): 'Zhenya died 28 Dec. at 12.00, 1941. Granny died 25 Jan. 3 in the afternoon, 1942. Leka died 17 March at 5 morn. 1942. Uncle Vasya died 13 Apr. 2 at night, 1942. Uncle Lyosha 10 May at 4 afternoon, 1942. Mummy 13 May at 7.30 morning 1942. The Savichevs are dead. All dead. Only Tanya remains.' A year later, Tanya also died of a hunger-related disease in the orphanage to which she was sent.

activity

Most people in Leningrad during the winter of 1941–42 had to survive on 125 grams of bread a day.
1 Weigh out 125 grams of bread on your kitchen scales.
2 How does this compare with the amount of bread you eat each day?
3 What do you eat each day apart from bread?
4 How do your answers help you to understand source 12?

The atomic bombs

You found out in Part 6 that hundreds of thousands of people were killed or injured in bombing raids on their towns and cities. Germany and Japan suffered the biggest losses when Allied bombers used 'area bombing' to create firestorms.

In the summer of 1945 the people of Japan were hit by a new horror. On 6 August 1945 an American plane dropped an **atomic bomb** on the city of Hiroshima. It exploded with a gigantic flash 570 metres above the city. The heat was so intense that people nearest to the explosion evaporated, leaving only their shadows on the ground. Tens of thousands were turned into charred corpses. Many who survived were very badly burned. Even more died later from radiation poisoning. Sources 13–16 help us to imagine what it was like to be in Hiroshima that day.

i An **atomic bomb** uses atomic energy instead of chemicals to make an explosion. The energy is produced when neutrons split the nuclei of an element such as uranium. This creates a very fast chain reaction which produces extreme heat and a massive explosive blast.

SOURCE 13

A street in Hiroshima two hours after an atomic bomb exploded over the city centre, three kilometres away. The photographer later died of his injuries.

SOURCE 14

This photograph, taken several weeks later, shows the damage done to the centre of Hiroshima by a single atomic bomb.

SOURCE 15

These paintings are by Tomoko Konishi, a survivor of the Hiroshima bomb. She did them in 1975 after seeing a television programme asking survivors to draw or paint their experiences. Along with hundreds of other survivors, none of them trained artists, she painted her memories so that future generations would not forget what had happened. The captions under each picture summarise what the Japanese writing says.

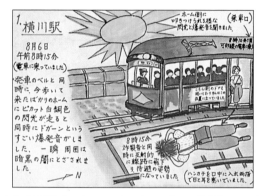

August 6, 1945. I got on a streetcar about 8.10 a.m. As I heard the starting bell ring I saw a silver flash and heard an explosion. Next moment everything went dark. Instinctively I jumped down on the track and braced myself.

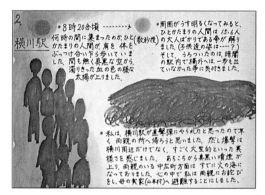

About 8.20 a.m. Soon the sun appeared blood red in the dark sky. Smoke was rising here and there. Nakahiro-cho where my parents lived was in flames. Apologising in my heart to my parents I decided to seek shelter.

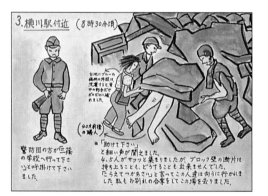

Around Yokogawa station about 8.30 a.m. I heard a woman saying in a small voice 'Please help me.' Four or five people got together to help her. But we couldn't lift the concrete block off her. Saying 'Forgive us' the others left her as she was. I prayed for her and then also left.

About 8.50 a.m. A lady about 40 years old was bleeding from her eyes. Unconsciously I wiped my face with my hands and I was surprised to see blood on them. I got my mirror out and looked into it. I found only a small cut on my eyebrow.

About 9.40 a.m. Refugees walked along the bank of the river. Everyone was in rags and hurt. I walked feeling guilty because I was not hurt. A woman was crying 'Can anyone help me?' The flesh of her side was scooped out and bleeding and I could see her ribs.

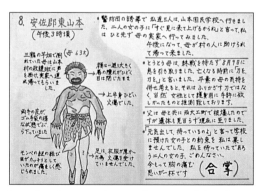

My mother. Her face was larger than usual, her lips were badly swollen. The skin of both her hands was hanging loose. The upper part of her body was badly burned. She passed away on August 9 before seeing the war end. My father disappeared and we never found the body.

More than 78,000 people were killed and 40,000 injured by the atomic bomb at Hiroshima. Three days later, a second atomic bomb exploded above the city of Nagasaki, killing another 40,000 people. The Japanese government did not know that the Americans had no more atomic bombs left after that. They surrendered on 14 August 1945.

Was there an alternative to the atomic bombs?

The atomic bombs had horrible effects. Was it really necessary to drop them? Was there not a less damaging way of defeating Japan?

One alternative was for Allied forces to invade Japan and fight the Japanese army in battle. Sources 16–18 show what they might have faced.

SOURCE 16

The total strength of the Japanese army was estimated at about 5 million men ... The Air Force Kamikaze, or suicide attacks ... had already inflicted serious damage on our seagoing forces ... There was a very strong possibility that the Japanese government might decide upon resistance to the end ... The Allies would have been faced with the enormous task of destroying an armed force of five million men and five thousand suicide aircraft ... We estimated that if we were forced to carry this plan to its conclusion, the major fighting would not end until the latter part of 1946 at the earliest. I was informed that such operations might be expected to cost over a million casualties to American forces alone.

Henry Stimson, US Secretary for War in 1945,
writing in an article in *Harper's Magazine* in 1947

As well as the Japanese army, the Allies would have to fight millions of civilians who had joined a defence force to protect their country from invasion. Kasai Yukiko, a high school pupil in 1945, later remembered what her teacher told the class to do if the Allies invaded:

SOURCE 17

When they do [invade] we must be ready to settle the war by drawing on our Japanese spirit and killing them. Even killing just one American soldier will do. You must be prepared to use the awls [carpentry tools] for self-defence. You must aim for the enemy's abdomen. Understand? The abdomen! If you don't kill at least one enemy soldier, you don't deserve to live.

Thomas R. H. Havens, *Valley of Darkness. the Japanese People in World War II*, 1978

1 Describe in your own words what happened to Tomoko Konishi (source 15).
2 If Tomoko could have taken photographs of what she saw at the time, do you think they would tell us anything that these pictures do not?
3 I could find only one photograph taken in Hiroshima on 6 August 1945 (source 13) to put in this book. Suggest why there don't seem to be more.

SOURCE 18

A Japanese soldier trains members of a 'People's Volunteer Corps' in the use of bamboo spears to defend their country against an Allied invasion, summer 1945.

activity

1 Look at sources 16–19.
a How can these sources be used as evidence that there was no alternative to using atomic bombs against Japan?
b Are you convinced by this evidence? Explain your answer.
2 Admiral Leahy (source 21) referred to 'bombing with conventional weapons' (i.e., non-atomic bombs).
a Use the information on page 79 to describe the effects of 'conventional bombing' on Tokyo.
b How was conventional bombing similar in its effects to atomic bombing?
c Look at source 23. How can this map be used to support the point of view in sources 21 and 22?

This wasn't the only danger facing the Allied forces. Several hundred thousand soldiers and civilians were prisoners of the Japanese. As one prisoner later wrote (source 19), an Allied invasion of Japan could have meant death for many of them:

SOURCE 19

For me, selfish as it may sound, there was the certain knowledge that if the bomb had not been dropped . . . Field-Marshal Terauchi [a leading Japanese commander] would have fought on and hundreds of thousands of prisoners in his power would have been killed. Even if we had not been deliberately massacred, we were near our physical end through lack of food.

Laurens van der Post, *Night of the New Moon*, 1970

Many of the American war leaders feared that an invasion of Japan would bring about the deaths of millions of soldiers, prisoners of war, and civilians. They wanted, therefore, to defeat Japan without invading it. As one of the war leaders later told journalists:

SOURCE 20

Any weapon that would bring an end to the war and save a million lives was justified . . . It was our duty to bring the war to an end at the earliest possible moment.

James Byrnes, US Secretary of State, in an interview in 1965

Not all the war leaders agreed with this view. Admiral Leahy, Chief of Staff to the US President in 1945, later wrote in his memoirs:

SOURCE 21

The use of this barbarous weapon at Hiroshima and Nagasaki was of no material assistance in our war against Japan. The Japanese were already defeated and were ready to surrender because of the effective sea blockade and the successful bombing with conventional weapons.

Admiral William Leahy, *I Was There*, 1950

And a Japanese war leader later said in an interview:

SOURCE 22

We were prepared to stage the decisive battle on the Japanese mainland . . . We thought we would be able to defeat the Americans on their first landing attempt. But if the Americans launched a second or third attack, first of all our food supply would run out. We didn't have a sufficient amount of weapons, nor could we have made more. Therefore if the Americans chose to come without haste the Japanese forces would have eventually had their arms up without the Americans resorting to atomic bombs.

Saburo Hayashi, secretary to the Japanese War Minister in 1945, interviewed in 1963

SOURCE 23

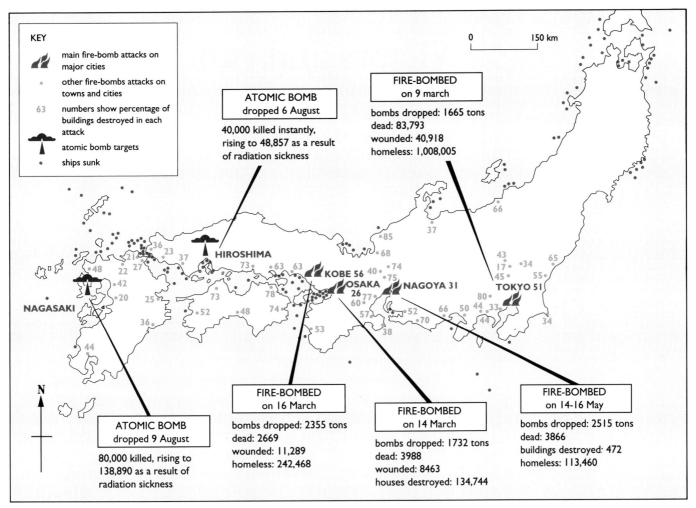

KEY

🔥 main fire-bomb attacks on major cities

• other fire-bombs attacks on towns and cities

63 numbers show percentage of buildings destroyed in each attack

☁ atomic bomb targets

• ships sunk

0 ——— 150 km

ATOMIC BOMB
dropped 6 August

40,000 killed instantly, rising to 48,857 as a result of radiation sickness

FIRE-BOMBED
on 9 march

bombs dropped: 1665 tons
dead: 83,793
wounded: 40,918
homeless: 1,008,005

ATOMIC BOMB
dropped 9 August

80,000 killed, rising to 138,890 as a result of radiation sickness

FIRE-BOMBED
on 16 March

bombs dropped: 2355 tons
dead: 2669
wounded: 11,289
homeless: 242,468

FIRE-BOMBED
on 14 March

bombs dropped: 1732 tons
dead: 3988
wounded: 8463
houses destroyed: 134,744

FIRE-BOMBED
on 14-16 May

bombs dropped: 2515 tons
dead: 3866
buildings destroyed: 472
homeless: 113,460

NAGASAKI   HIROSHIMA   KOBE 56   OSAKA   NAGOYA 31   TOKYO 51

N

assignments

At least fifty million people died in the Second World War.

1 Using the information in this chapter, list the main causes of death.

2 Which caused the greatest numbers of deaths?

3 Far more civilians than soldiers were killed in the war. Give as many reasons as you can to explain why this was so.

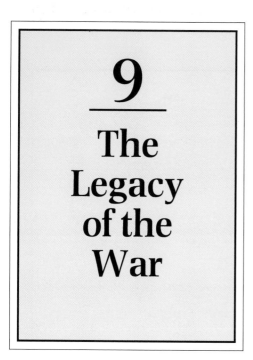

9

The Legacy of the War

Victors and vanquished

The Second World War ended in 1945 when first Germany and later Japan surrendered to the Allies. The Allies then occupied both countries and took steps to ensure that neither could fight again.

How Germany was treated

The Allies began by splitting Germany into pieces. As source 2 shows, eastern Germany was given to Poland. The rest was divided into four zones, each occupied by an Allied army. Berlin, the capital, was also split into four sectors. Austria was separated from Germany and split into four zones.

In Germany, thousands of Nazis were put on trial for crimes committed during the war. The most important were tried before an International Military Tribunal at Nuremburg. Of the twenty-one top Nazi leaders on trial, ten were hanged and seven given long prison sentences for 'crimes against peace and humanity'.

Next, the Allies made the Nazi Party illegal. They expelled thousands of Nazis from government jobs. They took control of the press, radio and film industry and made sure they did not put across Nazi ideas. They sacked Nazi teachers from schools and replaced Nazi textbooks with newly written books containing democratic ideas. In such ways the Allies 'de-Nazified' Germany.

How Japan was treated

Japan was occupied by an American army led by General MacArthur. Under his command Japan's armed forces were disbanded. Arms factories were taken apart. Two hundred thousand people who had supported the war were sacked from government jobs. Over a thousand politicians and army leaders were arrested and the main suspects tried for war crimes. Seven, including two former Prime Ministers, were found guilty and hanged.

After disarming Japan in this way, MacArthur changed the way the country was governed. Elections for a new parliament were held. The Emperor had to give up his claim that he ruled with god-given authority, although he was allowed to stay as leader. Censorship was abolished. Japan thus became a democratic country.

New frontiers

Germany was not the only country whose frontiers changed at the end of the war. Changes took place in many states in both Europe and Asia.

The new Europe

When Germany surrendered in 1945 the Allies controlled most of Europe. As source 1 shows, 12 million Soviet troops controlled eastern Europe. Four million troops from the USA, Britain and other western Allies controlled western Europe. This gave the Allied leaders – Churchill, Stalin and Roosevelt – the power to decide the future of most of Europe.

They had already decided what to do early in 1945 when they held a conference at Yalta in the Soviet Union. At the Yalta Conference, Churchill, Stalin and Roosevelt agreed that Germany must give up all its armed forces and be occupied by Allied armies.

SOURCE 1

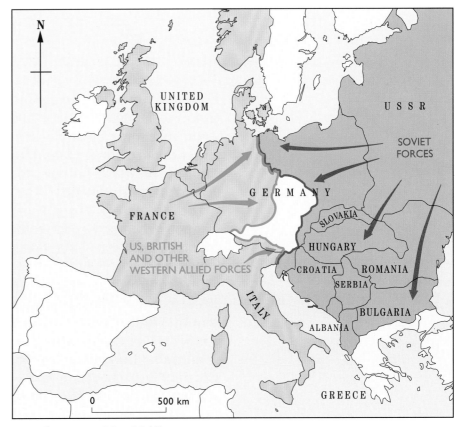

Map of Europe in May 1945.

SOURCE 2

Map of Europe
1945–49.

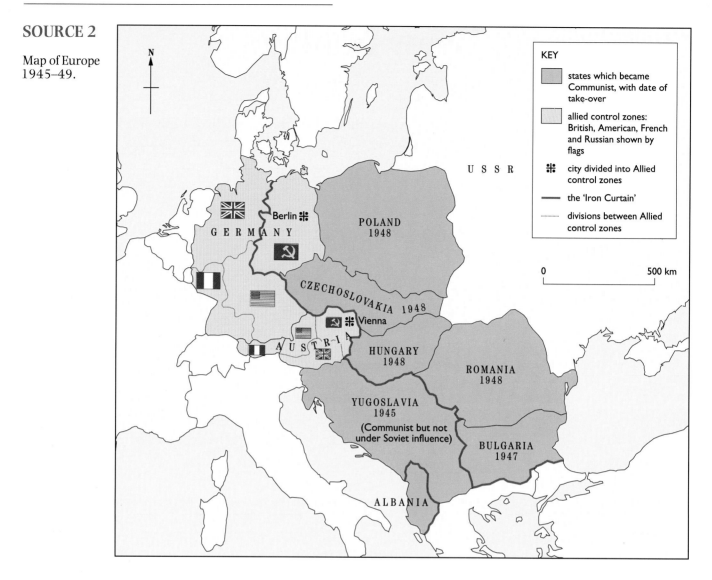

The Allies would take goods and machinery from Germany to help repay the damage to their own countries. They agreed that Poland would take some land from Germany and give some land to the Soviet Union (source 2). And they agreed that the liberated countries of eastern Europe should hold free elections to set up democratic governments.

The first two of these agreements were put into effect but the third was not. When new governments were set up in eastern European countries, the Soviet forces made sure that **communists** got the most important posts. Then they helped these highly-placed communists to take control of the press and the police. They also interfered in elections to stop non-Communists from winning. As a result, all the countries under Soviet control had communist governments by 1948, just like the Soviet Union.

Winston Churchill criticised these actions in a speech in 1946. He said that 'an iron curtain' had been drawn down between eastern and western Europe. The Communist governments which the Soviet Union helped set up behind the Iron Curtain would stay in power for the next forty years.

ℹ️ **Communists** believe that the people of a country should own and have equal shares in property, industry and business. In Communist countries only one party is allowed – the Communist Party – and its officials run the government.

The new Asia

i Nationalists aim to govern their own affairs in their own nation, free from foreign rule.

Before the war much of the Far East was under European control. As source 3 shows, 590 million people in India, Indo-China and the East Indies lived in colonies owned by Britain, France, Holland and Portugal. Many of them disliked European rule and joined nationalist groups which aimed to make them independent.

The war helped the **nationalists**. As you read in Part 4, Japan took over most of the European colonies in south-east Asia in 1942. The Japanese ruled them even more harshly than the Europeans they replaced. This made the nationalists even more determined to be free when the war ended.

In India, which the Japanese could not conquer, nationalists had been struggling for years to be free from British rule. They did not want to help the British war effort and did all they could to make the British leave India. The Japanese took advantage of their feelings. Using propaganda posters like source 4, they encouraged Indians to rebel against the British.

By the end of the war in 1945, nationalist feeling was strong throughout south-east Asia. So when the Europeans returned to their colonies to take back control from the Japanese, they were not welcomed. Nationalist groups fought them for control. As source 6 shows, they won. Five years after the end of the war, nearly all the colonies were independent.

SOURCE 3

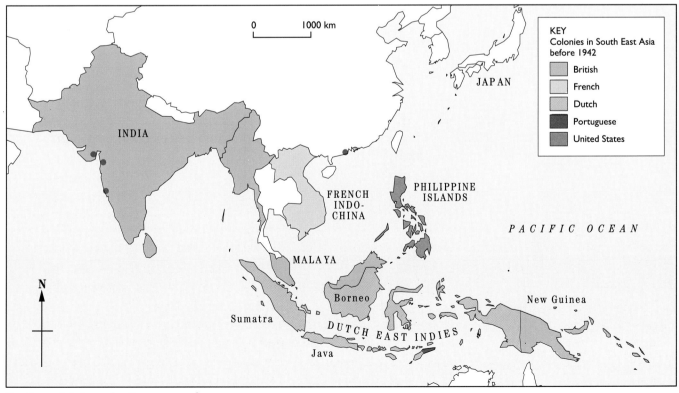

KEY
Colonies in South East Asia before 1942
- British
- French
- Dutch
- Portuguese
- United States

South-east Asia under European rule.

activity

1 Look at source 4.
a What did the artist want Indians to think about the British?
b Why do you think the Japanese sent posters like these into India?
2 Compare source 3 with source 5. How did the countries of south-east Asia change during the ten years after the Second World War?

SOURCE 4

This poster was dropped on India by Japanese planes in 1942. It shows Indians working as servants for a British officer. Servants in the background are rebelling against another officer. The writing, in Hindi and Bengali, says 'All British colonies are awake. Why must Indians stay slaves? Seize this chance – rise.'

SOURCE 5

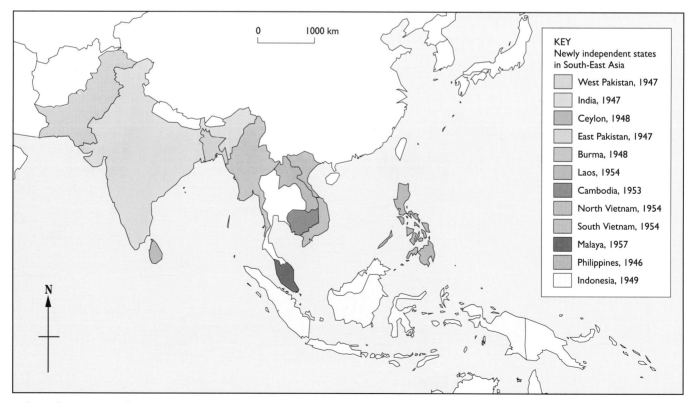

KEY
Newly independent states in South-East Asia

West Pakistan, 1947
India, 1947
Ceylon, 1948
East Pakistan, 1947
Burma, 1948
Laos, 1954
Cambodia, 1953
North Vietnam, 1954
South Vietnam, 1954
Malaya, 1957
Philippines, 1946
Indonesia, 1949

Independence in south-east Asia, 1945–55.

The Cold War

As you have read, the countries of eastern Europe were dominated by the Soviet Union after 1945. Churchill said that an 'iron curtain' divided them from western Europe.

The leaders of western Europe and the USA were suspicious of this. They feared that Stalin, the Soviet leader, would use his armies to get hold of more of Europe. Stalin, on the other hand, mistrusted the USA and Britain. Both the USA and Britain had long disliked the Communist system of the Soviet Union and both now had atomic weapons. He feared they would use these to destroy Communism.

This mistrust between the USSR and the USA and Britain quickly deepened. In 1947 the Americans decided to give aid to countries in which Communists were trying to take control. The Marshall Plan, as this aid package was called, said that the USA would give money to any country in Europe that needed help to repair war damage. The thinking behind this was that people were less likely to support Communism if they were well-housed and well-fed.

Seventeen countries in western Europe asked for aid and, over the next three years, received 13.75 billion dollars from the USA. The countries in eastern Europe did not receive any. Stalin thought Marshall Aid was an American plot to get more power in Europe and would not let them have anything to do with it.

By 1948 relations between the countries of the east and west were extremely bad. Both sides were building up their armies and stocks of atomic weapons. Both were spying on each other and both were using propaganda to criticise each other. People called this deep hostility between them a Cold War – a conflict in which the two sides opposed each other in every way short of armed force.

SOURCE 6

The Cold War between the Communist east and the 'Democratic' west is reflected in this photograph taken in Berlin in 1950. A tram leaves the American sector of West Berlin and enters Soviet controlled East Berlin. The notice on the left says that this is the 'end of the Democratic sector of Berlin.'

An Allied poster of 1942 shows the flags of countries which signed the United Nations Declaration at the start of that year.

The United Nations

The development of the Cold War created major problems for a new peace-keeping organisation set up at the end of the war. It was called the United Nations Organisation and it replaced the old League of Nations.

Origins of the United Nations

The United Nations was first thought of in a secret meeting on board a ship in the Atlantic Ocean in 1941. The meeting was between Winston Churchill, Prime Minister of Britain, and Roosevelt, the United States President. The purpose of their meeting was to discuss the future of the world after the war was over. The outcome was a declaration which they called The Atlantic Charter.

In the Atlantic Charter, Roosevelt and Churchill described their 'hopes for a better future of the world'. Their main hopes were that:

- all countries would have democratic governments;
- all countries would trade freely with one another and be prosperous; and
- all countries would reduce their weapons.

Several months later, Roosevelt suggested that all the Allied countries at war with the Axis powers should be called The United Nations. Twenty-six countries agreed with his suggestion. On 1 January 1942 they signed a United Nations Declaration saying that they agreed with the Atlantic Charter. During the next three years of war they grew in number as more and more countries joined the Allies. By 1945 there were fifty of them.

The United Nations Charter

Representatives of the fifty countries met in San Francisco in April 1945 and set up a full-time organisation to put the ideas of the Atlantic Charter into effect. They called it the United Nations Organisation and set out its aims in a document called the Charter. Source 9 shows the main aims of the UNO.

SOURCE 8

The purposes of the United Nations are:
1 To maintain international peace and security . . .
2 To develop friendly relations among nations . . .

activity

1 Look at source 7. What does the poster make you think about the United Nations? How does it create that impression?

2 Read source 8. How long after source 7 was the Charter written? Do the purposes of the United Nations seem different from the purpose shown in the poster?

3 To achieve international co-operation in solving international
   problems ... and in encouraging respect for human rights and for
   fundamental freedoms without distinction as to race. sex, language
   or religion, and

4 To be a centre for harmonising the actions of nations in the
   attainment of those common ends.

Charter of the United Nations, September 1945

Human rights and freedoms

As sources 7 and 8 show, one of the aims of the United Nations was
to give people freedom. This was based on an idea of President
Roosevelt. He had said in a speech in 1941:

SOURCE 9

We look forward to a world founded upon four essential freedoms.
The first is freedom of speech and expression ...
The second is freedom of every person to worship God in his own way.
The third is freedom from want ...
The fourth is freedom from fear.

Franklin D. Roosevelt, *Speech to the US Congress*, 6 January 1941

After the war was over, the United Nations wanted to carry on
fighting for such freedoms. In 1948 it made a Universal Declaration
of Human Rights. Roosevelt's four freedoms were listed in the
introduction to it. These were the main points of the Declaration:

SOURCE 10

1 *All human beings are born free and equal in dignity and rights ...*
2 *Everyone is entitled to all the rights in this Declaration ...*
3 *Everyone has the right to life, liberty and security ...*
4 *No one shall be held in slavery or servitude ...*
5 *No one shall be subjected to torture or cruel treatment ...*
7 *All are equal before the law ...*
9 *No one shall be subjected to arbitrary [unlawful] arrest, detention*
   or exile.
11 *Everyone charged with a penal offence [is] innocent until proved*
   guilty according to law in a public trial ...
18 *Everyone has the right to freedom of thought, conscience and*
   religion ...
19 *Everyone has the right to freedom of opinion and expression ...*
20 *Everyone has the right to freedom of peaceful assembly ...*
21 *The will of the people ... shall be expressed in periodic and genuine*
   elections which shall be by universal and equal suffrage.
23 *Everyone has the right to work [and] equal pay for equal work ...*

United Nations Universal Declaration of Human Rights, 1948

activity

3 During the Second World
War millions of people were
deprived of the rights listed
in source 11. Give examples
of people who were
deprived of their rights. In
each example, say which
right was taken away and
how this was done.

SOURCE 11

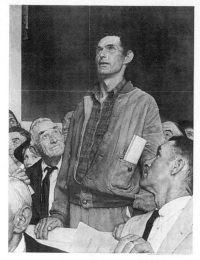

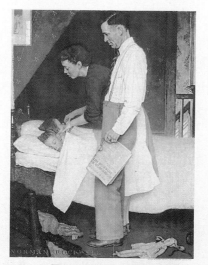

OURS... to fight for

Freedom of Speech

Freedom of Worship

Freedom from Want

Freedom from Fear

American artist Norman Rockwell painted these pictures to illustrate Roosevelt's 'four freedoms'. They first appeared in the *Saturday Evening Post* in 1943 and became so popular that they were widely reproduced in posters like this.

All the members of the United Nations signed the Declaration of Human Rights, but it was only a voluntary agreement. The UN did not have the power to make countries give their citizens all the rights in the Declaration. Source 12 gives an idea of how many have done so since 1948. It is based on information collected by Amnesty International, an organisation which investigates and tries to stop abuses of human rights around the world.

SOURCE 12

Some human rights violations in the early 1990s, according to information collected by Amnesty International.

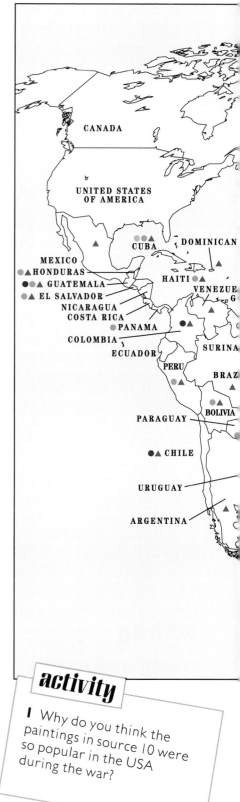

activity

I Why do you think the paintings in source 10 were so popular in the USA during the war?

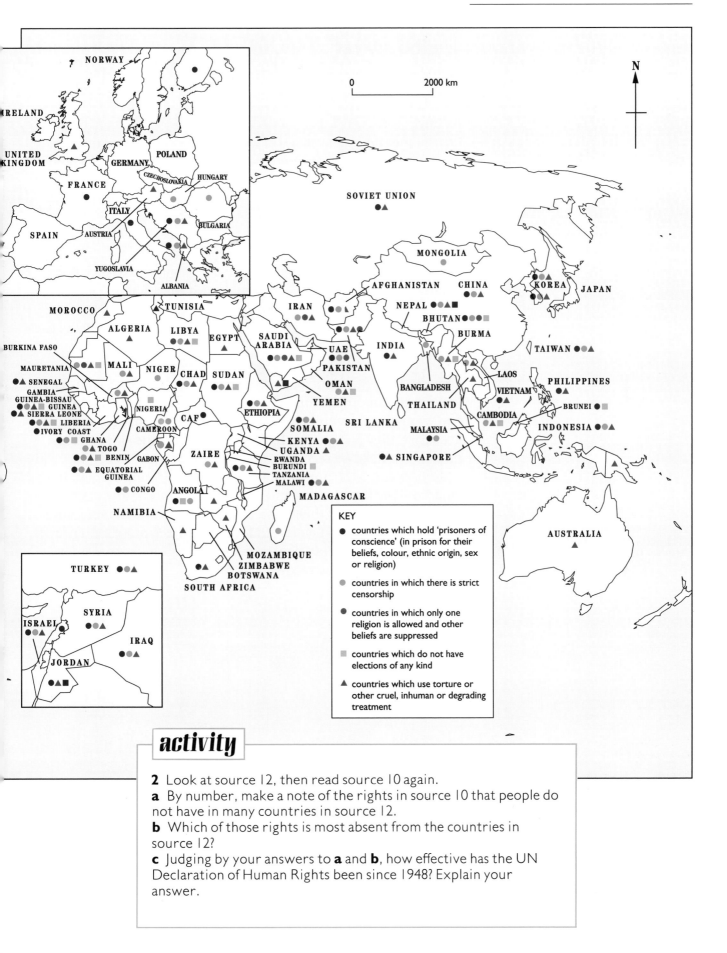

KEY

● countries which hold 'prisoners of conscience' (in prison for their beliefs, colour, ethnic origin, sex or religion)

● countries in which there is strict censorship

● countries in which only one religion is allowed and other beliefs are suppressed

■ countries which do not have elections of any kind

▲ countries which use torture or other cruel, inhuman or degrading treatment

activity

2 Look at source 12, then read source 10 again.

a By number, make a note of the rights in source 10 that people do not have in many countries in source 12.

b Which of those rights is most absent from the countries in source 12?

c Judging by your answers to **a** and **b**, how effective has the UN Declaration of Human Rights been since 1948? Explain your answer.

Postwar recovery

As soon as the war was over people started to repair the damage to their homes and their places of work. The biggest rebuilding jobs were in Japan, Germany and Britain, whose cities had been bombed.

How Japan recovered

Japan in 1945 was in ruins. Two million people were dead. Four buildings out of every ten had been destroyed by bombs. Industry was at a standstill and 13 million people were out of work. There was no oil. Most of the country's ships had been sunk. Millions faced starvation.

Yet, as source 14 suggests, the Japanese soon repaired the damage. Four things helped them do so. First, the Americans gave Japan huge amounts of money. They were thinking of the future and wanted a prosperous country to trade with. So, over the next five years, they poured two billion dollars of aid into Japan. This helped its industries recover.

Second, the government changed Japan's farming system. It took land from the landowners and sold it to peasants at low prices. Now that they had land of their own, the peasants worked harder and grew more food than before. And as they earned more money from selling their crops, they spent more on factory-made goods. This, too, helped industry to recover.

SOURCE 13

Led by former soldiers, Japanese children in late 1945 carry bags of building sand up a river bank near Tokyo. Children in the background are filling more bags.

SOURCE 14

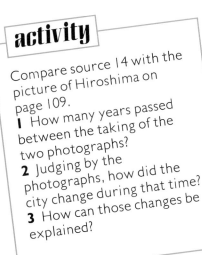

activity

Compare source 14 with the picture of Hiroshima on page 109.
1 How many years passed between the taking of the two photographs?
2 Judging by the photographs, how did the city change during that time?
3 How can those changes be explained?

The main street of Hiroshima in 1952, shortly after the end of the American occupation.

Third, the Japanese worked very hard. As source 14 shows, even children joined in the task of rebuilding. But people not only worked hard. They were also ready to accept low wages, so employers could spend their profits on new machinery rather than on pay rises. And although they did not earn high wages, many workers saved money in banks. This meant that banks had lots of money to lend to business people to rebuild factories.

How Germany recovered

Like Japan, Germany in 1945 was a ruined country. In the British zone, for example, nearly half of all houses were damaged beyond repair. A third of the coal mines were too damaged to produce coal. Only 1,000 out of 13,000 kilometres of railway track could be used. Rivers and canals were blocked. There was no petrol.

A large part of Germany recovered quickly. For example, the military government which ran the British zone quickly organised a massive rebuilding programme. Former Nazis were put to work clearing rubble. Every able-bodied person was made to do building work (source 15). Schools were set up to train women as carpenters, electricians, painters, plumbers and bricklayers.

The eastern zone of Germany, run by the Soviet Union, recovered less quickly than the western zones. The Soviet Union had been badly damaged in the war. To help repair the damage, the Soviet authorities took huge quantities of machinery and raw materials

SOURCE 15

Teams of German women like this cleared millions of bricks from bombed buildings in 1945.

from their zone of Germany. This made it very difficult for the Germans to repair their own war damage.

In 1949 the occupation of Germany came to an end. Originally, the wartime Allies had agreed that Germany should have one government. But as the Cold War developed, Russia disagreed with the others about what kind of government this should be. After a long dispute with Russia, the USA, Britain and France decided to go ahead alone. They combined their three zones of Germany to form the 'Federal German Republic' in the west. The Russians in the east set up a 'German Democratic Republic' with a Communist government. Germany remained divided into two countries for the next forty years until a revolution in East Germany allowed the country to be reunited.

How the Allies recovered

The two leading Allies who won the war recovered from it in very different ways.

The United States recovered quickest. No part of the USA had been bombed or occupied, so there was no war damage to repair. And as you have read, many unemployed Americans got jobs making war materials. In 1945 millions of workers started spending their wartime earnings when factories switched from making war materials to **consumer goods**. This led to an economic boom and the American people were soon the richest in the world. Source 16 gives an idea of how rich some Americans became in the postwar years.

i **Consumer goods** are things like food, clothing or household equipment that people use or consume in their daily lives. They are different from goods produced as part of another manufacturing process. For example, sheets of steel are not consumer goods but motor cars made from steel are.

Britain was the only Allied country which fought both Germany and Japan from the very start to the end of the war. As a result, Britain in 1945 was in bad shape. Factories, docks, mines, railways and roads were worn out. The government owed £3,000 million to other countries. Earnings from trade had dropped to less than half their pre-war level.

The only way Britain could recover was to earn more money by selling things to other countries – machinery or cars, for example. This also meant buying fewer things from abroad. One result of this was that the British people after the war went through a period of 'austerity' in which they had to go without all sorts of things. Some foods and materials were rationed even more strictly than in wartime. Bread, which had never been rationed during the war, was rationed from 1946 to 1948. Coal and other fuels were as scarce as they had been in wartime. Housing was in short supply. So, while many Americans grew rich in the postwar years, most British people had to put up with continued shortages.

activity

Look at sources 16 and 17.
1 What do the pictures tell you about Britain and the USA in the postwar years?
2 How can the differences between the two be explained?

SOURCE 16

This photograph was published by *Life* magazine in 1951. It shows a factory worker, Steve Czekalinski, and his family, with the amount of food an average American family ate in a year.

SOURCE 17

People queue to buy coke for their fires in London in 1947. Some have brought old prams and hand carts to carry the coke home in.

Britain's need to earn more from exports led to another problem. Some of the country's main industries were out-of-date and unprofitable. They were already obsolete before the war and now they needed to be modernised or replaced. But this could not be done at the same time as increasing exports. Many old-fashioned coal mines, steel works, shipbuilding yards and textile works therefore stayed in business. Although this succeeded in increasing exports, it meant that Britain was much slower than the USA, Germany and Japan in making its industry efficient and profitable. In future years, as a result, those countries were to become richer and more modern than Britain.

assignments

The Second World War changed many things. The world after the war was very different from the way it had been in 1939. Some of the things which changed were:

- the government of Germany (see pages 20–21, 114 and 126)
- governments in Eastern Europe (page 116)
- the nations of south-east Asia (pages 117 and 118)
- relations between the USA and western Europe, and the USSR and eastern Europe (pages 116 and 119)
- international cooperation (pages 120 and 121)
- cities and towns in Germany, Britain and Japan (pages 119, 125–126)
- the Jewish population of Europe (pages 99–105)
- employment (pages 17, 24, 74, 77 and 125–126)

1 Divide a page into two columns headed 'Before the war' and 'After the war', then make brief notes under those headings to show how each thing in the above list changed. For example:

	Before the war	After the war
The government of Germany	A dictatorship governed by Hitler and the Nazi Party from 1933–45	Governed by Allied armies from 1945–49, then divided into two countries 1949–89

2 Your list shows three different *kinds* of changes: political changes, economic changes and social changes. Group the changes under those three headings.

3 Some of the changes in your list made life worse for millions of people. Some of the changes improved life for many others. Choose two changes which you think made life worse and two which were improvements. In each case explain your answer.

4 Which of the things in your list do you think brought about the greatest changes in the world? Explain your answer.